Contents

OUTDOORS WITH YOUNG PEOPLE

A leader's guide to outdoor activities,
the environment and sustainability

By

Geoff Cooper

Illustrations by Mary Higgins ('Dodgy')

Russell House Publishing

First published in 1998 by:
Russell House Publishing Limited
4 St. George's House
The Business Park
Uplyme Road
Lyme Regis
Dorset DT7 3LS

© Geoff Cooper
© Illustrations Mary Higgins

British Library Cataloguing-in-Publication Data:
A catalogue record for this manual is available from the British Library.

ISBN: 1-898924-24-4

Text design and layout by TW Typesetting, Plymouth, Devon

Printed by Cromwell Press, Trowbridge, Wilts.

Dedication

This book is dedicated to my Dad who loved the outdoors and who turned even the simplest walk into an adventure.

About the author

Geoff Cooper is head of Metropolitan Wigan's two outdoor education centres in the Lake District. He has introduced many young people to the outdoors through a range of experiences based on adventure, field studies, problem solving, conservation and the arts and regularly runs training courses for youth leaders and countryside staff. He has organised workshops on environmental education for teachers and leaders in Britain and across the rest of Europe.

Acknowledgements

The idea for this book came from a training course for outdoor leaders I helped to organise with Scottish Natural Heritage in 1996. Talking to other outdoor leaders convinced me that we can become powerful ambassadors for the environment. What we sometimes lack is the confidence to harness our skills, knowledge and enthusiasm.

Writing a guidebook to encourage leaders seemed a simple project but it turned out far from a straightforward journey. There were many stopping places and uncertainties en route. Fortunately, the opportunity to spend time outdoors with young people, experiencing, enjoying and learning about the environment constantly rekindled my interest.

Many people have given help and support in writing this book. I would like to thank Ken Ogilvie for his thoughts on the initial idea and John Gittins and Lorna Cooper for their many comments during the draft stages.

Some of the ideas have been inspired by working with friends on environmental workshops in a variety of European countries. Thanks go to Bryan Edmondson, Phil Sixsmith, Veta Tsaliki, Andrea Déri, Julie Cox, Alberto Martinez Villar, John Gittins, Alexander Georgopoulos and Richard Lemmey. There have also been many benefits from working with colleagues at Low Bank Ground, Coniston and trying out activities with leaders and young people visiting the centre over the years.

I would also like to thank Terry Gifford, Berlie Doherty, Lorna Cooper, Sandi Stevens, Bryan Edmondson, Phil Sixsmith and David Scott for providing case study material. Late in the day, Mary Higgins ('Dodgy') came to my rescue with a fine selection of sketches and I must not forget my young son, George, who quickly transformed my rough diagrams to something a lot more presentable on his computer.

Photographs
Page 5 Terry Gifford
All other photographs Geoff Cooper

Introduction

Without the mass involvement of young people caring for their environment there is no hope of sustainability or halting the loss of environmental quality.

Sir Crispin Tickell

Who is the book for?

It is for leaders who are taking young people into the outdoors and who wish to use these experiences to encourage environmental awareness and more sustainable lifestyles. The term 'outdoor leaders' is used throughout the book to include many different types of leaders for example, youth and community workers, countryside and urban rangers, teachers, outdoor centre and field study centre staff, Scout and Guide leaders and Duke of Edinburgh Award leaders. Their goals may be related to education, recreation, personal or social development. This does not matter, as long as there is an interest to learn in, about and for the environment.

The book is not aimed at the expert or specialist but at all leaders who have an interest in the environment and who wish to extend their knowledge and skills. It provides a simple framework for understanding environmental education and sustainability and many practical ideas and activities to use with young people.

How this book will help leaders

The outdoors is the source of much enjoyment and inspiration. The book offers leaders many ideas to help young people enjoy and appreciate the environment. It should also give leaders confidence in introducing environmental education. Outdoor leaders are in a special position and their actions can help change attitudes and behaviour. Through their work they can address the following concerns:

1. There is a need for all of us to have a different approach to the earth and its people. If the people on this planet are going to survive with a reasonable quality of life then we must be more sensitive to the environment and adopt more sustainable ways of living.
2. Young people are interested in environmental issues. Many wish to know the causes of problems and some are prepared to take action to protect or

improve an environment. There is also a concern about poverty, malnutrition and the distribution of wealth throughout the world.

3. Many outdoor leaders are interested in the environment. They appreciate that an awareness of the environment can often enhance the outdoor experience and that direct experience of real-life situations in the outdoors can contribute significantly to environmental education.

4. Outdoor centres and clubs may also be interested in developing their leaders' environmental understanding for organisational reasons. For example, the use of environmental activities can ease staffing ratios and provide low risk alternatives in adventure-based programmes.

5. National governing bodies for outdoor activities, such as canoeing, sailing, orienteering and mountaineering, are showing an increasing interest in environmental matters. Until now this has usually been confined to encouraging codes of environmental conduct rather than presenting opportunities for encouraging appreciation. These bodies are influential, they control training and qualifications and there is great scope for promoting environmental considerations in their agendas.

The outdoors is on our doorstep

You do not need to trek miles or travel into remote areas to enjoy and appreciate the outdoors. There are a growing number of organisations offering opportunities for adventurous and creative activities in and around the city. There are relatively wild areas close to most people's homes—old quarries, canal banks, waste ground, woods, old industrial sites, parks, allotments, city farms—and many urban areas are richer in wildlife than parts of our countryside. There are larger open spaces, such as country parks, near the edge of many cities and most young people living in urban areas are only a short bus or train journey away from more extensive areas of moorlands and mountain.

It is important for young people to experience wild landscapes and dramatic scenery but leaders should not neglect opportunities on the doorstep. There are many examples of community action and environmental improvements in towns and young people should be encouraged to take part in these projects. Most of the ideas and activities in this book can be applied to any environment. Although starting on the doorstep outdoor programmes should try to make connections between personal, local, national and global environments.

Young people, society and the planet

Many outdoor leaders will be aware of the problems facing young people in a rapidly changing society. We live in a society divided by education and wealth. An increasing number of young people fail in our education system and find themselves on the outside, dispossessed. Our prevailing culture measures success in terms of material possessions. The growth of unemployment, homelessness and crime and the break-up of family life are some of the obvious signs of social disintegration. Many sections of the population are disaffected, they are failures in the present system, they are not valued and often they can gain recognition only by confronting the system which has dispossessed them.

Young people leaving school face many uncertainties. They are encouraged to consume; to strive for glamour, speed, excitement. These can only be achieved through well-paid jobs. Yet for many these jobs are not available. Does our education system address any of these issues? Are we educating young people to feel at home in a society where there are fewer opportunities for work? Are we challenging an economic system based on greed and growth and which is failing to support the basic needs of a section of our people and others on the same planet?

The same process that has produced these social and economic upheavals in Britain is provoking ecological uncertainty at a global level. We are consuming the Earth's resources at an unsustainable rate and through our greed and waste we are threatening the global systems we depend upon. Our abuse of the rainforest and the oceans arises from the same system that disregards global poverty and the needs of the under-privileged in our own society.

There is a lack of purpose in many people's lives. We have become removed from the natural processes of living. We insulate ourselves from the rhythms of nature, from the seasons, from day and night, from the land and sea, from other life. We surround ourselves with surrogates, second-hand experiences, vicarious pleasures. These are poor compensations for feeling part of the planet, for having a spiritual connection, a kinship with the Earth. There is a need to reconsider our lives, to look for ways of living which are not to the detriment of other people or harmful to ecosystems. We need to redefine 'quality of life' and adopt more sustainable lifestyles. Education, both formal and informal, has a vital role to play in creating a new vision for the future.

The role of outdoor leaders

Outdoor leaders have a special role in educating for a changing society. They work informally with young people in the outdoors beyond the constraints of home and classroom. Often motivation is higher and there are opportunities to build confidence and self-esteem. They can create a climate where young people succeed.

Leaders offer direct experiences of the environment through activities such as adventure, field studies, art or conservation. A key element is learning through enjoyment. These activities have great potential in helping to encourage environmental awareness, understanding and action. Developing feelings for and knowledge of the environment can add interest, enrich the experience and even act as a therapy for some people. Experiencing simpler lifestyles in the outdoors can also introduce ideas about alternative ways of living and question the prevailing values of society.

Sometimes leaders lack confidence in introducing environmental activities. There is a feeling that they need to be scientists and be able to name plants and animals and explain the complex relationships between them. This book firmly dispels this notion. Environmental awareness and understanding often come from direct and positive experiences in the outdoors, they are as much to do with feelings as to do with scientific knowledge. Outdoor leaders have many personal, social and organisational skills and use methods ideal for encouraging environmental education. It is important they appreciate their advantages.

Finding your way round the book

The book is divided into two sections. The first section puts the work of outdoor leaders into context. It provides a framework for understanding environmental education and sustainability and gives leaders the background to learning, leadership, the school system and the value of outdoor education. The second section builds on this framework and offers many ideas, activities and examples of good practice. It considers the whole range of environmental education from awareness and understanding through to action.

This simple structure should allow the leader to dip into the book with ease and there is no reason why some of the activities should not be tried first and put into context later. Some activities are designed for use with the young people whereas others are more appropriate as training exercises for leaders themselves. A selection of guidelines is offered in point form throughout the book and I hope these will be useful as a basis for discussion in training sessions.

I am convinced that outdoor leaders have much to offer environmental education. Enjoyment of the outdoors encourages young people's interest and appreciation of the environment. Leaders can motivate their groups and help develop many of the personal and social skills necessary for more sustainable lifestyles. I hope this book gives leaders the confidence and inspiration to make the links between their work and the quality of young people's lives in the future.

A Framework for Good Practice

1. From environmental awareness to sustainability

Getting to grips with environmental education

Although the term environmental education was only introduced in the 1960s, in Britain its development can be traced to earlier environmental thinking in natural science, rural studies, fieldwork, countryside conservation and urban studies. It is commonly accepted that environmental education should include opportunities for learning *about*, learning *in* or *through* and learning *for* the environment. For example, it is possible to learn from a book about the relationships between the geology and landforms in a mountainous area. This is an important basis for developing a body of knowledge but in itself is not environmental education. Learning can also take place through first-hand experience in the environment, for example, by travelling through a mountainous area or by investigating relationships between landforms by measuring and mapping in the field. Learning in the environment can extend knowledge, develop understanding and encourage skills such as observation, recording and problem solving. But it is also important to appreciate the value of landforms, how certain landscapes are threatened and how we can help conserve them. If we simply study the landscape to gain knowledge of its formation or to practise skills this is not environmental education. There is a key area of education missing which relates to feelings, attitudes and values and is ultimately concerned with our action for the environment.

Getting to grips with environmental education.

It is clear from this that environmental education is a process of learning rather than a subject. Its aims can be expressed as:

- To provide opportunities to acquire knowledge, values, attitudes, commitment and skills needed to protect and improve the environment.
- To encourage the study of the environment from a variety of perspectives— physical, geographical, biological, sociological, economic, political, technological, historical, aesthetic, ethical and spiritual.
- To arouse awareness and curiosity about the environment and encourage active participation in resolving environmental problems.

National Curriculum Council, 1990

Educating *for*—A word of caution

Over recent years environmental education has become more action oriented. Education *for* the environment has become a rallying call for those wishing to effect change in society and promote more active participation. This viewpoint has now even been accepted throughout formal education.

The Canadian educationist, Bob Jickling (1992) warns us of the danger of this. He reminds us that education is about enabling people to think for themselves. He argues that: 'in a rapidly changing world, we must enable students to debate, evaluate, and judge for themselves the relative merits of contesting positions'. The term 'education for' implies that there is a prescribed outcome, it is more in line with training than with education.

I have some sympathy with this view, we should be cautious of the terms we use and their implications. Environmental education is political, it is about change but not by following prescribed agendas. If this were the case there would be a danger of this process of learning being hijacked by governments to meet their own goals. Rather it is education which encourages understanding, critical skills and clarification of values so that young people can play an active part in change towards a more environmentally conscious society.

A simple model

These aims are far reaching and it is helpful to have a framework to appreciate this process of learning. We can consider environmental education as made up of five elements.

1. *Awareness*. This includes awareness of our own connections with the environment as well as awareness of environmental issues. Raising awareness through feelings and personal response is a neglected area of environmental education and yet it may hold the key to changing our behaviour.
2. *Knowledge*. Environmental education is underpinned by a body of knowledge which includes understanding ecological relationships but also understanding how we can be involved in decision making through our own political and social system. We need to answer two questions: How are we connected to ecological systems? What can we do to improve this relationship?
3. *Skills*. A range of skills are necessary, from scientific skills of observation, recording and analysis to more fundamental skills of effective communication. Personal and social skills which relate to taking individual and group responsibility for environmental action are also invaluable.
4. *Attitudes and values*. Encouraging positive attitudes is essential for environmental education. Attitudes can be developed through experiencing a personal link with the environment and can also be explored through critical thinking about issues. As leaders we can help clarify values but we should recognise the need for independence of thought and respect for evidence.
4. *Action*. Environmental education is about change, it is about improving our relationship with the planet and it should inevitably lead to personal and group action. This can include changes in our own behaviour, such as reducing our dependence on cars or saving water. It can relate to practical conservation, for example creating a wetland habitat or restoring a building. It can also involve political action, such as lobbying, joining a pressure group or taking direct action. Environmental education has failed if it does not lead to beneficial changes in our behaviour and lifestyles.

These five elements summarise the process of environmental education. They can be seen as a series of stages starting with awareness and leading to action. This is a logical progression but all the elements are interrelated and it is possible to start at any point (see figure 1.1.). For example a field-studies approach may start with the skills of collecting information and analysing it. This could lead to awareness of an issue and further fieldwork to gain evidence or knowledge of the situation. Such investigation may lead to

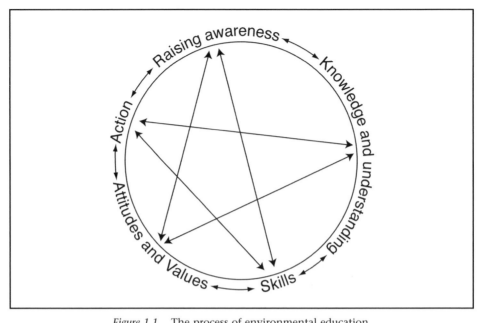

Figure 1.1. The process of environmental education

changes of attitudes and an attempt to seek a solution to the problem. In contrast, we might start the process with action for example with a practical conservation project. The task of cleaning up a stream may provoke questions on how the pollution occurred and this awareness and knowledge could lead to discussions of our attitudes and values and may lead to changes in our own behaviour.

All five elements are important in environmental education. Formal education often concentrates on knowledge and skills and in the past has not given enough attention to developing personal feelings, clarifying attitudes and encouraging personal responsibility. Outdoor leaders are in a good position to develop these aspects.

Linking personal, social and environmental education

It is clear from the above model that there are close links between personal, social and environmental education. The significance of these links for outdoor education was first outlined at a landmark conference at Dartington in 1975. The report on outdoor education suggested that the most important aims are to heighten awareness of and foster respect for:

- *self*—through the meeting of challenge
- *others*—through group experiences and the sharing of decisions
- *natural environment*—through direct experience

Developing this relationship, Colin Mortlock (1984) sees adventure education as 'an awareness of, respect for, and love of *self* balanced against

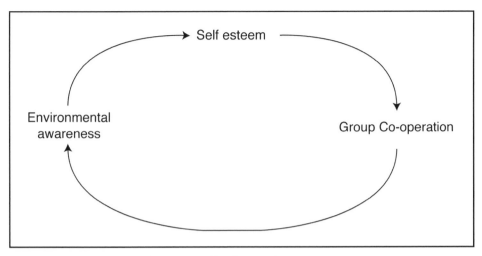

Figure 1.2. Self, others and environment

an awareness of, respect for, and love of *others* balanced against an awareness of, respect for, and love of the *environment'*. Extending this, I think that personal, social and environmental aspects are inseparable and all part of the same process. A person who has little self-respect or self-esteem is unlikely to work well in a group or to have respect for the environment. If we accept this then our work in raising confidence and self-esteem may be the very foundation required for environmental education. Success in co-operating with a group and direct, personal experiences of the environment can enhance self-esteem and lead to an upward spiral of achievement (see figure 1.2).

The following story helps to illustrate the link between personal, social and environmental awareness:

Case study—South Walney

We had come on a day visit to South Walney nature reserve off the Cumbria coast to see thousands of nesting herring gulls, lesser black back gulls and eider ducks. Our small group of eleven year olds had to tread carefully to avoid trampling the nests. Even on the well-marked trails we had difficulty in avoiding the nests with their exquisitely camouflaged eggs. At first the group were interested in the behaviour of the birds but after a while they became tired of looking at the eggs and the birds squawking overhead. One or two of the group were restless and quarrelsome and wanted to explore away from the directed route.

After lunch we reached the shore. It was low tide. A huge expanse of sand with shallow pools stretched before us. In a flash shoes and socks were off and we were all running rapidly towards the sea. The children were surprised at the changes in the texture of the sand; the hard ripples under their feet, the deep, soft sand where they sunk up to their ankles and the lovely pools of warm water. We ran faster and faster towards the water's edge, then slumped in the sand under a perfect blue sky. This was a wild, exciting place. There were imaginary deltas and sand-dune deserts. It was another world, miles away from anywhere.

On the way back across the nature trail, something had happened to change the group. They were more alert, more interested in what was around them, they were closer to each other. They collected 'treasures', special stones rounded by the waves with minerals glistening, periwinkles, razor shells and driftwood. They wanted to show them, wanted us to share them and answer questions.

What had produced the change? It was the need for play, for spontaneity, for adventure. A chance to feel the natural environment through their bodies, to release the tensions of the disciplined nature study they had experienced in the morning. To run, skip, jump and feel the freedom of a wild area, a new and uncertain environment. The niggles and quarrels of the morning evaporated. The children had enjoyed a common experience, they had come together, there was a sense of achievement. Now was the time for the teacher to build on the enthusiasm and motivation and help them to understand the significance of this special environment.

This story reminds us that there is a strong link between personal, social and environmental education. We cannot expect an interest in and respect for the environment if there is little self-esteem or respect for other people. Positive experiences in the countryside, in this example through adventure, can encourage this process.

Activity—Environmental statements

This activity can be used as a basis for discussion with other outdoor leaders.

Below there are 12 statements relating to environmental education. Put each statement on a scale of 1 (strongly agree) to 5 (strongly disagree).

Of the statements with which you agree or strongly agree which can you tackle most easily in the outdoors?

Compare your assessment of the 12 statements with the list of characteristics of environmental education given below.

Statements on environmental education

Statement	1 – 5 rating

1. Environmental education is about changing attitudes, values and patterns of behaviour.
2. Environmental education is cross-curricular and relates to all areas of the curriculum.
3. Feelings are as important as knowledge in encouraging positive attitudes to the environment.
4. Environmental education is a life long process and involves both formal and informal education.
5. Direct experience of the environment is essential for environmental education.
6. Environmental education should relate to both local and global issues.
7. Environmental education should encourage people to take action for the environment.
8. Knowledge of political and social systems is essential for environmental education.
9. In environmental education we should concentrate on the main problems facing the future of the planet.
10. Self esteem and co-operation are the basis of environmental education.
11. Active and participatory learning is the most appropriate method for environmental education.
12. Environmental education requires a basic understanding of ecology.

Characteristics of environmental education

- It is a process of learning that involves raising awareness, gaining knowledge and understanding, developing skills, clarifying attitudes and values and taking action for the environment.
- Its aim is to encourage people of all ages to adopt more sustainable lifestyles.
- It is cross-curricular—the arts, social sciences and science all have their part to play in educating for the environment.
- It is a lifelong process and can be encouraged through formal and informal education.
- Personal, social and environmental awareness are part of the same process and essential to environmental education.
- The most appropriate teaching and learning methods are those that encourage active participation and responsibility. Learning through first-hand experience, enquiry, group discussion, role play and personal reflection are as important as more traditional methods.

- An environmentally aware citizen will show creativity, an ability for critical analysis, decision making, futures thinking and reasoned judgements as well as a love and concern for nature and an empathy to others.
- It is concerned with personal, local and global dimensions.

There is no such thing as an 'environmental' problem

It is common to talk of environmental problems. Some are seen as big problems, issues that affect the whole planet, such as global warming or ozone depletion. Others affect large regions such as the acid rain across many parts of northern Europe. Some so-called environmental problems are national or local issues such as large road building schemes, suburban shopping developments or loss of wetland habitats. Whatever the scale, none of these are 'environmental' problems but problems caused by people, by us. They are problems produced by our demands for particular lifestyles, for example the desire for new cars, cheap food and entertainment and leisure. Calling them 'environmental' helps to remove the onus from the real causes. It helps us to feel less responsible. Environmental issues are simply social, economic or political problems in disguise.

Activity—Trace that problem

1. During an outdoor activity introduce an issue facing the local environment. Examples might be: river or lake pollution, loss of

---

ancient woodland, plans to build a new road or the removal of hedgerows.
2. Give the group time to consider and ask questions about the issue whilst outdoors.
3. Back at base divide the group into smaller groups of three or four persons. Ask them to write the issue in the centre of a large sheet of paper, then write the possible causes on the paper connecting them with lines to the issue. These causes, in turn, may be affected by other causes that can be linked with further lines.
4. Ask a member of each group to comment on their findings. It may surprise some of the participants how an issue can often be traced back to certain root causes related to our own lifestyles. An example is shown in Figure 1.3.

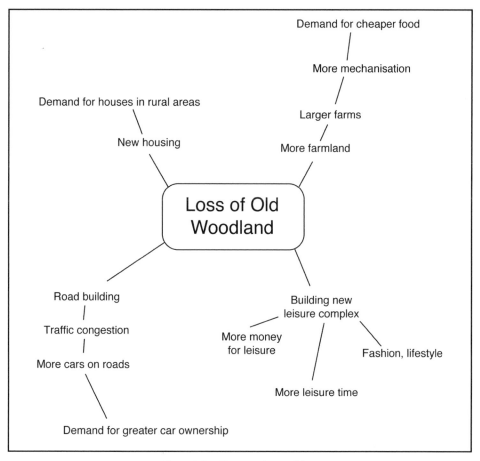

Figure 1.3. Tracing the problem

Towards sustainability

With the recent international interest in sustainability, environmental education has taken on an even more action-oriented focus. As a result I think our role as outdoor leaders is more significant.

There have been many attempts to define sustainability. An early definition and one often quoted is: 'development that meets the needs of the present without compromising the ability of future generations to meet their needs' (Brundtland Report, 1987).

This definition was a starting point but is now considered to be too narrowly centred on the needs of people. More recent definitions have stressed the importance of improving the quality of our lives without harming the ecosystems we depend upon.

Sustainability is not just about environmental protection but also includes sharing resources more equitably and improving the quality of our lives in terms of access to health care, education, justice, work, leisure and democracy. Sustainability relates to people from all sections of society and countries of the world. It is concerned with both present and future generations. It implies the need for a new ethic based on co-operation rather than competition, quality of life rather than standard of living and community rather than individual interest. Education must play a key role in changing attitudes and behaviour. Outdoor leaders can play a significant part in this process.

Sustainable development

The term 'sustainable development' is commonly used, especially by politicians and there is a danger that it means all things to all people. It is a contradiction since 'sustainability' implies that there are ecological limits which are currently being exceeded, whilst 'development' implies economic growth and maintaining the *status quo*. Sustainable development is acceptable to many governments and business interests because it registers their 'concern' but still allows them to follow growth policies. It is a good badge to wear.

The difference between the two concepts of 'sustainable development' and 'sustainability' is best shown through an example. The former accepts current lifestyles and attempts to manage their impact by technological advances. The latter questions our need for growth and proposes alternative lifestyles. The differences can be shown through attitudes to the car. The 'sustainable development' approach argues for lead-free petrol, catalytic converters and recyclable components whereas the 'sustainability' approach questions our use of the car and looks at alternative modes of transport.

I find the use of the term 'sustainable development' confusing and contradictory and will try to avoid using it in the book.

What is a sustainable community?

What does a sustainable community look like? Here are a few suggestions:

1. Everyone is provided with the basics for a healthy life—food, clean air, water, shelter, education, medical care.
2. Bio-diversity is encouraged through habitat protection and careful use of land and water.
3. There is an emphasis on reducing consumption and waste and re-using and recycling energy and materials.
4. Activities are organised through participation at a local level.
5. There is regional self-sufficiency and less need for transport.
6. Public transport is given higher priority.
7. There is a 'sense' and 'spirit' of place. Natural and cultural environments are cared for and celebrated.

Educating for sustainability

How do we educate for such a change? It is clear that education for sustainability is a wider concept than environmental education and also includes aspects of personal and social education, citizenship, economic understanding and moral and spiritual considerations. A model for such an education is shown in figure 1.4., the framework of which is based on the three simple considerations:

1. I recognise the **need** to act—*Awareness*.
2. I **know how** to act—*Empowerment*.
3. I **will** act—*Commitment*.

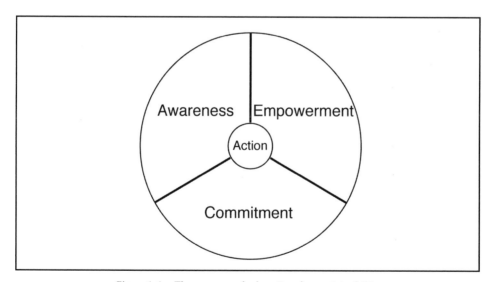

Figure 1.4. The process of educating for sustainability

Let us consider these a little further.

Awareness
There are two aspects of awareness. It is important to have a knowledge and understanding of issues influencing the environment and our quality of life.

For example it is necessary to have some ecological understanding to appreciate the intricate relationships between plants, animals and ourselves. But it is also vital to have knowledge of political structures to appreciate how and why decisions are made which influence these relationships. So we can understand that the removal of hedgerows means a loss of habitats for a range of insects, birds and small mammals but we also need to understand that this environmental issue has been produced by underlying economic considerations such as the need to obtain higher crop yields from greater mechanisation allowed by large fields. Ironically, I went through school with no knowledge of ecology or political and economic understanding—the very basis of understanding my relationship with life on the planet.

The second aspect of awareness is concerned with feelings and having a personal connection with the environment. We have become separated from nature, we think of ourselves as apart from rather than a part of nature yet our minds and bodies still respond to rhythms of day and night, lunar cycles and the changes of the seasons. There is an urgency to develop this biological awareness through encouraging a personal response to the environment. Understanding comes through feelings as much as knowledge. This aspect of awareness could be the key to attitude and behavioural change.

Empowerment

How many times do we hear young people say that 'they' make the decisions for us? 'They' could be the government, the council, the planners, business, in other words faceless bureaucrats as opposed to us, the people. There is a need to involve young people, to give them responsibility and make them feel responsible for their own lives, to empower them.

A basis for such empowerment is to develop self esteem, confidence and motivation. Many young people have poor self worth, they have failed in a school system designed to measure a particular type of intelligence and academic learning. They are given little responsibility in this system, there is a lack of identity and motivation is low. The first step is to reverse this process, to develop self esteem and to improve confidence.

Empowerment also involves encouraging a range of skills and competencies. Effective communication is essential but for many oral literacy may be more important than the written word. Interpersonal skills are increasingly important in an age when knowledge can be acquired at the press of a button. Problem solving, lateral and critical thinking and negotiation will be valuable to young people involved in decision making. Creativity and vision for the future are also required to inspire positive change. These skills are often underdeveloped at school. Knowledge of ecological and political systems also forms a prerequisite for empowerment.

Commitment

Sometimes we are aware of an issue that needs addressing, we have the ability and confidence to take action but we still do not do anything about it. What triggers our commitment to act? This is a difficult question, we may change our behaviour because there are rewards or penalties. Rewards may be economic, but they may also come from the satisfaction that we are improving the quality of life for ourselves or others. Good self esteem, tolerance, empathy and co-operation are attitudes conducive to action. Young people who do not value themselves or respect and co-operate with others are unlikely to show concern for the environment. Penalties such as fines or prosecution can alter behaviour, for example the dramatic shift in attitudes towards drinking and driving in Britain over the last 20 years. There is evidence to suggest that the development of personal feelings and strong connections with an environment will influence our commitment to act for its protection.

Awareness, empowerment and commitment are the building blocks leading to action. We can summarise the necessary knowledge, skills and attitudes that are essential in educating for a more sustainable society.

Ten essential competencies

1. Self esteem, confidence and motivation.
2. Co-operation, trust and empathy.
3. Communication skills, including negotiation and decision making.
4. An ability for critical thinking, lateral thinking and problem solving.
5. Self reliance, the ability to take responsibility.
6. Futures thinking.
7. Feelings of belonging to the natural world.
8. Creativity, imagination and a personal response to the environment.
9. Knowledge of ecology and social and political systems.
10. An ability for reflection and evaluation.

This list is not comprehensive but gives an indication of some of the important skills and qualities needed to change the present situation. A quick glance at this list and many outdoor leaders will realise they are very much on home territory! We have long recognised the value of social and personal skills and know that these have not met with much success in formal education. Generally schools do not encourage creativity, problem solving and leadership, common outcomes of many outdoor education programmes.

We will return to these competencies in a later chapter when we consider how outdoor programmes can be designed to encourage more sustainable lifestyles.

Activity—From our own backyard to the tropical rain forest

The terms 'environmental education' and 'sustainability' can be confusing because they encompass so many aspects of our lives and also involve different scales from the personal level through to global considerations. Consider the following activities and how they relate to the models outlined above:

1. Helping to plant trees on a derelict urban site.
2. Learning about the 'greenhouse effect'.
3. Bird watching.
4. Saving on our use of water.
5. Taking part in a debate on plans for a new road.
6. Watching the sunrise from the mountains.
7. Buying fair trade goods from the Third World.
8. Taking part in a Food Chain game.
9. Investigating freshwater ecology through pond dipping.
10. Studying the causes of tropical deforestation.
11. Writing a letter to your MP to support public transport.
12. Doing a survey of what people value in their town.

All of these activities relate to environmental education. Try recording each activity according to the two scales: Personal—Local—Global and Awareness—Understanding—Action shown in Figure 1.5. For example, 'Bird watching' is about awareness at a personal level whereas 'Buying fair trade goods from the Third World' relates to global action.

	Awareness	Understanding	Action
Personal			
Local			
Global			

Figure 1.5. Grid for recording environmental activities

This helps us to appreciate the nature and extent of environmental education. As outdoor leaders it may be much easier to contribute to personal, and to some extent local, awareness and understanding. It is likely to be much more difficult to tackle global issues and encourage action at all levels. This draws our attention to the possible limitations of our work but we should look for opportunities to encourage global thinking and action.

2. The value of outdoor experiences

How is the outdoors used to encourage learning?

Leaders use the outdoors in a variety of ways to encourage learning. A few of the more important types of outdoor education are considered in the following points.

1. *Adventurous activities*. These can relate to the development of physical skills and may be part of a physical education programme. They can also be concerned with personal, social and environmental awareness or simply provide opportunities for leisure. They can include activities such as canoeing, climbing, mountain walking and orienteering.
2. *Field studies*. These are usually related to subjects such as geography or science as part of the school or college curriculum. Young people are introduced to fieldwork to develop investigative skills and extend their knowledge and understanding of a topic.
3. *Problem solving*. These activities are used to develop specific personal or team skills. They often form part of a structured activity which involves planning, doing and reviewing.
4. *Aesthetics and environmental awareness*. The outdoors can be used as a stimulus for feelings and personal response. This may involve sensory activities, observation, reflection, writing, drawing, sculpture, dance or drama.
5. *Practical conservation*. Here the emphasis is on learning practical skills to carry out a project to improve the environment.

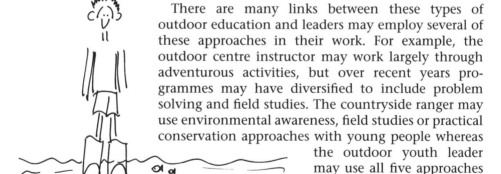

There are many links between these types of outdoor education and leaders may employ several of these approaches in their work. For example, the outdoor centre instructor may work largely through adventurous activities, but over recent years programmes may have diversified to include problem solving and field studies. The countryside ranger may use environmental awareness, field studies or practical conservation approaches with young people whereas the outdoor youth leader may use all five approaches in their work.

The outdoors can be used as a stimulus for feelings and personal response.

Common elements

Although the aims of the various types of outdoor learning may be different there are common elements. All are concerned with active learning in the outdoors, they involve young people learning by doing. This learning may be experiential if it is seen as part of a process that involves reference to previous knowledge and experience, planning, reviewing and building on each new experience (this is considered in the next chapter). This is a powerful form of learning which affects personal and social development and can have many implications for environmental education.

Case study—The benefits of outdoor learning

Many claims have been made about the benefits of outdoor education. Research in different countries has suggested strong links between outdoor adventure and aspects of personal and social development. David Hopkins and Roger Putnam (1993) explore some of these links in their book, *Personal Growth Through Adventure*. There is a wealth of anecdotal evidence which supports the importance of outdoor experiences. As an example we can consider results from two surveys of the impact of outdoor experiences for young people based at two residential centres during 1993/4.

Low Bank Ground and Hinning House are outdoor and environmental education centres in the Lake District owned by Metropolitan Wigan Education Authority. Young people, from urban areas, aged from 9 to 18 years, come to the centres for a five-day outdoor education programme linked to their school curriculum. The work of the centres involves all five types of outdoor education outlined above although the emphasis is on adventurous activities, problem solving and environmental awareness. The aims of the centres are expressed in terms of personal, social and environmental education.

In the first survey teachers were asked to state their objectives for their visiting groups. Seventy-three schools returned questionnaires and the majority mentioned two or more objectives.

Over 85% of the responses referred to opportunities for personal and social development. Of these the most frequent statements were: the development of new personal skills in the outdoors (33%); opportunities for team building and group co-operation (31%); the development of personal qualities, particularly confidence, self esteem and self reliance (25%) and opportunities to develop the 'whole' person (8%).

More than 45% of all the questionnaires made some reference to the importance of the environment. Of these responses the most common statements were: the opportunities gained from exploring new and contrasting environments (43%); the chance to encourage environmental awareness (40%) and the opportunity to experience dramatic and beautiful environments (9%).

Some 34% of all the responses also mentioned the opportunities given by the centres to extend classwork as part of the National Curriculum. Geography, science, PE and art were the subjects most frequently cited and environmental education and citizenship the main cross-curricular links.

It is clear from this that many teachers recognise that outdoor experiences can help in delivering aspects of the National Curriculum but they have an even more important role in providing for the development of the whole person through personal, social and environmental awareness.

A second survey was conducted by the centres in the form of a letter to teachers who had visited the centre with groups in the past asking for examples of how young people had benefitted from their experiences. Thirty replies were received and this proved a useful addition to existing anecdotal information.

These letters give evidence that many of the teachers' stated aims are met.

Personal and social development
Many comments relate to personal and social development. For example:

> In just a week we had grown together, caring, loving but misunderstanding. Like a family, good times and bad times. But never forgetting. (Loraine, aged 15)

For many children a visit to the outdoor centres is a watershed in their lives. They show a wide range of emotions and learn how to deal with them either privately or with the aid of their companions.

During their visits children learned to become self-reliant ... the reference to teamwork became more than just words, pupils became so much more aware of the need for co-operation in all forms of activity and enjoyed the satisfaction this type of behaviour can bring.

Children often see each other and the staff with new eyes and with increasing tolerance.

Self-esteem, confidence and behaviour
References to the development of self-esteem and confidence and the consequent changes in motivation and behaviour are common.

It is clearly hard to attribute changes in students' behaviour specifically to experiences at one of the centres. That these contribute significantly to some students and their development is incontrovertible. A student with special needs (emotional problems), came to us in Year 9 not having completed a year's education. She proved to herself that she could meet the challenge of the mountains and consequently grew in confidence. She later went on holiday on her own to another outdoor centre and left school last summer with ten GCSE grades A–C.

Watch a child develop confidence as she inches her way up a rock climb ... I could fill a book with the success stories I have personally witnessed over so many years.

Achievement
It is also common for children who under achieve at school to benefit from an outdoor programme where a range of different skills are developed.

Children who do not have an academic leaning can often come to the fore and gain much in self-esteem from their ability to cope.

A number of quiet, shy children have gained a lot of confidence ... this has greatly helped their achievement back at school.

Equal opportunities
References are frequently made to children who would not normally have the opportunity to gain these experiences.

We have a number of children who would not normally be able to experience the natural beauty of the Lake District, whose parents make the effort to enable their children to go.

Only a handful of our children have ever visited such beautiful countryside and even fewer have had the chance to canoe, climb and explore in these areas.

Environment
The influence of such environments on children is a continual theme.

In the outdoors children gain a much greater appreciation of the environment. I believe the environment has a profound affect on them.

There is a much greater awareness of children to those behaviours that have a direct effect on the environment.

They begin to appreciate nature around them and its importance. They realise they are only a small cog in the wheel.

A course allows students to experience landscapes of outstanding natural beauty or rich industrial heritage. The light and atmosphere of these landscapes changes continually with the weather. Outdoor sessions even in inclement weather can provide strong stimuli for art and design. The visual language of pattern, shape, form, tone, colour and texture are all demonstrated in a direct, immediate and enjoyable way.

The groups experience beauty, there is a sense of wonder which may lead to concern and action to protect the environment.

Students look at their home areas in a different way; sometimes they see pollution, traffic problems but also environments that can be improved.

Curriculum links
The letters support the objectives expressed by the teachers in terms of the potential of outdoor programmes to develop and enhance the school curriculum.

Outdoor courses give valuable insights into studies in Geography and Science and help to deliver Environmental Education as a cross-curricular theme.

The children make many comparisons between the two environments—home and away—and are able to make judgements upon the suitability of these environments to their needs.

We have used the outdoor centres to provide the 'outdoor and adventurous activities' as part of the PE curriculum and for work in Geography on contrasting localities.

Outdoor education as a catalyst

Outdoor education can trigger change, stimulate new interests and inspire young people. There are many examples of how young people have followed up experiences:

> Dave and Darren attended a large comprehensive school near the centre of Wigan. Their course at Low Bank at the age of 15 was their first visit to the Lake District. One day the following summer they arrived on motorbikes laden with a tent and other camping gear. 'Where can we put our tent?', they asked with enthusiasm, 'we're going to the mountains tomorrow.'

Many children return to the Lake District or introduce activities to mums, dads, grannies and grandads. Some come back to the centre others return to sites such as Grizedale Forest to see the sculptures or take a boat out on Coniston Water. Dawn came with a special needs group several years ago and has returned regularly with her parents despite now attending a special school in Scotland.

There is evidence to suggest that by becoming generally more confident and by gaining experience and knowledge of the countryside young people are given greater access to activities and environments. Outdoor experiences have an important role in this empowerment. There is an obvious link, here, with the concept of 'stepping stones', where positive experiences of new activities and environments open up opportunities in other areas. This role gains strong support in the letters survey:

> New interests are kindled. We have children who have been taken to the Lake District by their parents after visiting one of the centres. The experiences last in the children's memory for many years if not for a lifetime.

> A 12-year-old girl complained loudly during the fell walk, 'What have we come up here for?' A little after she returned home she purchased her own equipment and now regularly takes her parents and younger brother fell walking at weekends

There are many examples of children joining canoeing, orienteering and climbing clubs as a result of centre experiences. Some courses, such as Earthkeepers, an environmental programme, are started and completed in the school. Several letters commented not only on the extension of learning back in the classroom but also the 'cascade' effect on other children.

> Our visits to the outdoor education centres have become fundamental to our curriculum. Although not all children are able to attend there is a very real 'cascade' effect achieved informally through

conversation and discussion but also in a more structured way through display, assembly and group activities.

Following a Hinning House visit children were encouraged to ask questions such as: How can we improve our school environment? The result has been a link with the 'People and Places' project and all the children are involved in improving the school grounds.

Enthusiasm for outdoor education always pours over into the everyday life of the school with displays of photographs, collected materials, assemblies etc.

The sheer pleasure of living for a few days in such a beautiful environment exuded from the children's conversations for weeks after their return to school'.

Peak experiences.

It is clear that occasionally some young people are inspired through very intense experiences. These may occur through adventure, through a deep awareness of a natural environment or the development of new skills and group relationships. Sometimes there is an unlocking of talent, a realisation that some important change has occurred and an individual has grown richer as a result. Joy Palmer (1992) conducted a survey of 232 environmental educators and found that outdoor experiences have been a major influence in developing their interest in the environment. There is much anecdotal evidence for inspirational or peak experiences leading to new interests and changes in attitudes.

A young student-teacher recently visited Low Bank Ground as a leader with a primary school group. She had been to the centre ten years previously with her own primary school. Her memories of the week were incredibly vivid. On a recent meeting with three former classmates she said that each could remember their experiences of the course in surprising detail. She felt her own experience was a 'milestone' in her education and it had led to developing her interest in the environment'.

Such experiences may occur only once or twice in a lifetime and may be fundamental in triggering educational change. There is a growing interest in the impact of 'peak experiences' or critical events in education (see for example Peter Woods, 1993).

A culture for outdoor and environmental learning

During outdoor programmes visiting teachers work in active, open ways with the young people and clearly both teachers and students benefit from this positive and informal relationship. It was a common theme in the letters.

Whilst teachers have had the opportunity to observe, the children are also learning more about their teachers and a stronger relationship develops between the two.

So, without sentiment or exaggeration, we simply recorded what we, as teachers, saw ... students scattered in a woodland working in complete co-operation, building and forming natural sculptures, in absolute silence. Students, frozen in a biting lakeside wind, waving and celebrating each others' work. So, I think that as teachers, we too went on a journey and have discovered the fine quality of work which open-ended enquiry can create.

It is a unique teaching experience with all the members learning from each other.

There is little doubt that teachers need to build up their own confidence and knowledge in outdoor and environmental education. They return to the centres on in-service courses and may bring their students back on their own, independently organised, weekends. This confidence, interest and experience encourages teachers to develop outdoor learning opportunities near the school and in other areas. A 'culture' of outdoor and environmental learning develops and the children benefit enormously.

I have acquired the specialist skills and knowledge to be able to lead groups in all kinds of different activities and it has enabled me to start a mountaineering club ... I have been a part of this training both as pupil and teacher and the 'cascade' system has filtered through all areas of education.

These surveys provide evidence of the fundamental value of outdoor education for personal growth, social interaction and environmental awareness. Such case studies and research adds strength to the work of the Foundation for Outdoor Adventure (page 142) which promotes the values of outdoor and adventurous experiences for young people. This national organisation has produced a manifesto which emphasises many of the benefits recorded in the case study.

A manifesto for outdoor adventure

The Foundation for Outdoor Adventure published its manifesto in 1997. This recognises the importance of outdoor adventure in five areas of our lives:

1. *In education*—through developing personal qualities essential to the education of the whole person.

2. *In the social context*—through encouraging self-esteem and social skills, especially amongst disadvantaged young people.
3. *In business*—through developing self-reliance, flexibility and other competences and values identified by business.
4. *In the environment*—through appreciating the relationships between humanity and the total ecosystem and their own responsibilities towards a sustainable environment.
5. *In sport and recreation*—through encouraging a wide range of physically and aesthetically rewarding sports and active and healthy lifestyles.

The manifesto recognises the importance of lifelong learning that often results from well-structured outdoor experiences. The outcomes are holistic involving the development of the whole person- mind, body and spirit-for all aspects of life.

Young people, adventure and risk

Swallows and Amazons lost forever

Small worlds
blown up with
global awareness of
man's brutality.

Innocence
whitewashed with
the facts of life and
fear of strangers.

Imagination
boxed in with
packaged entertainment and
conformity.

Adventure
drowned with
life jackets and
the obligatory adult.

Smothered with expectation,
Strangled with caution,
Childhood has been taken care of;
Swallows and Amazons lost forever.

Lorna Cooper

As a society we are becoming obsessed with protecting children. Many parents are reluctant to leave their children alone out of doors. In Britain in

1971 80% of all seven and eight year olds went to school on their own, by 1990 this had dropped to just 9%. Practically all eleven year olds used to walk to school, now it is down to 56% and still falling.

Barry Hugill reported in the Observer (29 March, 1998) on research in Zurich in Switzerland which found that thousands of children are being kept indoors, like battery hens, because of parents' fears, largely of traffic. He argues that this could equally apply to any large British city. When these over-protected children start school they find it difficult to mix and show considerably less-advanced social and motor development. Behavioural problems are more likely as the children have not learnt to socialise and negotiate with their peers.

Over the last ten years the media has highlighted the risk from strangers. This has been reinforced by police visits to schools and campaigns and slogans to put young people on their guard from the threats that lurk at every corner. In fairness there have been abductions and horrific murders which have been blazened in the public's mind but they should be put in context. These dangers are miniscule and should be balanced carefully against the need to give young people the confidence and independence essential to growing up in a rapidly changing society.

Overprotection is insulating young people from the wider world around them. The child's universe is shrinking. Basic outdoor activities like going to the shops, crossing the road, building dens on waste land or playing in the local park are being denied or supervised by parents. The repercussions of this are enormous. There is concern about young people's health. The British Heart Foundation warns of a huge rise in heart disease in 20 to 30 years as a result of fewer children getting out and about. Perhaps even more significant is the fact that we are producing an inward-looking generation, less independent, less critical and more easily shaped by television and other forms of mass media. In the words of the poem above: 'Imagination boxed in with packaged entertainment and conformity'. Is this the breeding ground for critical thinkers and active citizenship?

There are strong arguments to suggest that we give young people too little responsibility. Jean Liedloff, a psychotherapist who spent several years living amongst the Yequana indians of Venezuela argues that children gain from the physical closeness of parents but also from opportunities to be self-reliant. She describes how the Indian children are naturally self protective, for example in handling sharp knives and swimming in fast rivers even at an early age. This is a vital part of their growing up and becoming full members of their society. The following short story reinforces the need to allow for independence and self reliance in our own culture.

Alternative Bonfires

It was Bonfire Night in the village. Crowds gathered in anticipation by the lakeshore, around the little booking office. A thick rope kept the viewers at least 100 metres from the fire. The members of the fire brigade in their uniforms and helmets busied themselves positioning fireworks on posts and fences. The fire was lit and a thousand rockets and firecrackers spread and sparkled across the night sky. The huge fire was ablaze but the distance was too great to feel the heat. Ben joined the queue for hot dogs and looked for his friends to have some fun. They had lost interest in the fire.

The next night we were at a party in the village. A bonfire had been carefully prepared in the large garden. The fire quickly spread its warmth. Everyone gathered round, it was communal and conversation came easy. Ben and his younger sister fed the fire with logs and branches. They felt the heat on their cheeks and the smoke in their nostrils. Occasionally they retreated into the cold night to take in blasts of fresh air but soon returned to re-stock the blaze. The adults were surprised at their level of interest and how much care they took in tending the fire. The youngsters felt responsible and they were learning rapidly through all their senses. They instinctively responded to potential danger and adjusted their actions. Above all it was their fire, they were not the passive observers of the night before.

Outdoor education is undeniably an effective way of encouraging confidence
and self reliance. It has, however come under attack from the same over
protective forces that are prevalent in society at large. In Britain there have
been ten deaths in outdoor education over the last ten years. This is an
extremely safe record considering the millions of young people who have
been introduced to outdoor activities. Compare this with the several
thousand road deaths that have occurred among young people over the same
period and it puts the actual risk into context. And yet outdoor organisations
have come under considerable scrutiny over the last few years. There is now
a licensing authority and regular inspections. As a result some organisations
are offering less adventurous activities. Other opportunities for young people
to experience and enjoy the outdoors are being lost because of the fear of
perceived risks and the resulting litigation if an incident occurred. The writer
and broadcaster, Libby Purves (1996), is vigorous in her support of the
benefits of outdoor education:

> A real expedition, in real wilderness, shows children the eternal reality beneath
> the thin skin of civilisation. It takes them beyond the shallowness of fashion and
> style to point out certain basic truths without which a great deal of history,
> literature and art will never properly touch them. It demonstrates that clothes
> are for warmth and protection first, that food is fuel, that cold and heat can kill
> you and that you have to watch your companions as closely as yourself.

The real risk to society is not about introducing young people to challenging
situations in the outdoors but about banishing a generation to the controlled
safety and apathy of their homes.

Benefits of outdoor education in educating for sustainability

Many of the benefits of outdoor education already discussed can make an
important contribution to educating for sustainability. This is because many
of the personal and social skills developed through outdoor programmes are
also those required to accept and adapt to change. Outdoor education also
encourages the clarification of attitudes and values and questions our
relationship with the environment. Some of the key benefits are now outlined.

Motivation
A key word in outdoor education is *success*. Many young people fail in formal
education and they may also fail at home and amongst their friends.
Motivation and success are common ingredients of outdoor learning. Young
people, in general, enjoy the outdoors, their level of interest is high and they
are more receptive to knowledge. Motivation also affects self esteem,
confidence and attitudes to others and to the environment.

Multiple intelligence
Most classroom learning is related to left-brain, logical or analytical thinking.
Some young people who are predominantly right-brain thinkers under-

achieve in schools. They are often regarded as less intelligent as their skills such as creativity, problem solving and leadership are not assessed in most school examinations. Their talent is frequently unlocked in outdoor education. It is common for leaders who know the ability of young people in formal situations to be surprised by their change in attitude and performance in the outdoors. Good outdoor education involves both left-brain and right-brain thinking and allows young people to develop their full potential. This range of skills and competencies is essential in educating for sustainability.

Personal responsibility
Outdoor education often places young people in situations where they have to take responsibility for their own actions. They may take responsibility for clothing, personal equipment and money and develop personal skills in the outdoors, such as those associated with observation, map reading, kayaking and recording information.

Co-operation
Learning in schools is usually based on competition. This may be appropriate to train a top class athlete or a Mastermind contestant but it is totally inadequate for educating for community living in a rapidly changing society. Teamwork and co-operation can be developed in many ways in the outdoors, for example through problem solving activities, group fieldwork and mountain expeditions. Outdoor activities can be designed to encourage trust, effective communication, negotiation and decision making. Such social skills are transferable and of fundamental importance to sustainable living.

Reconnecting
Outdoor education offers the opportunity to experience the natural world through mind, body and spirit. We often feel a 'sense of wonder', which can be inspired as much from a single dewdrop as an expanse of ocean. We begin to appreciate the interdependency of life on the planet. There is a chance to respond to the elements and natural rhythms, to rekindle a spiritual link which is within all of us. For some this reconnection may act as a therapy and it may, through releasing feelings, play a signicant role in gaining commitment for the environment.

Awareness of human impact
Experience of the outdoors helps us to understand the fragility of some environments and how our behaviour can have dramatic effects on the appearance of the landscape and its bio-diversity. Sometimes we can take simple measures to lessen our impact, for example by avoiding particular crags during nesting time or trampling hay meadows. This awareness of how we relate to the natural systems can enhance our own enjoyment and appreciation of the outdoors and may help us to 'tread more lightly' in other aspects of our lives.

Alternative lifestyles

Chris Loynes (1996) has argued that outdoor adventure is being packaged and commercialised and this process dissociates people from their experience of community and place. There is, however, the opportunity in the outdoors to experience a simpler, healthier and uncommercialised existence. Wild or quiet places can provide an antidote to mass culture with its five-minute soundbites. There is time to reflect, to put our lives into perspective, to consider our values. Outdoor leaders should be aware of pressures from commercialisation and through their own example encourage alternative lifestyles.

Real issues

Moving through the outdoors we confront real issues, for example there may be land use conflicts, such as the need to protect an ancient woodland threatened by a new road or the impact of a wind farm on a small rural community weighed against the benefits of renewable energy. Through activities such as fieldwork and drama we can begin to explore the complexities of such issues, appreciate the underlying social, economic and political pressures and make our own judgements. Enquiry and critical thinking skills are invaluable in educating for a changing society.

Plan, do, review

For many years there has been an interest in using the outdoors for personal development and team building. Problem solving activities are used as part of a development training process, which can be expressed in simple terms as planning, doing and reviewing. This process is relevant to all aspects of our lives and constant evaluation and planning helps us to cope with change.

3. Learning and leadership

Introduction

> Give a person a fish and you feed them for a day. Teach a person how to fish and you feed them for life. Teach a person how to learn to fish and they don't need a fishing teacher. Teach a person how to learn and they don't need a teacher.
>
> Chinese Proverb

How young people learn in the outdoors is as important as what they learn. If leaders are trying to encourage a particular range of skills, attitudes and behaviours which are relevant to a more sustainable lifestyle they need to consider their role as a leader and the process of learning. The quality of learning in the outdoors will relate to:

- leadership
- teaching and learning methods
- the activities
- The environment.

It is important that all of these are in harmony and working to produce the desired outcomes.

Advantages of outdoor leaders

Youth leaders, rangers, outdoor and field-centre staff have a number of advantages over teachers working in more formal settings such as schools and colleges. It is worth reminding yourself of these benefits as it can help to boost your confidence:

- You are usually liked. You have a good image.
- You have novelty value. Unlike teachers you are not seen regularly from week to week.
- You do not have the constraints of a formal curriculum, exams, timetables or the bell.
- You have a knowledge of particular environments which are rich resources for learning.
- You have enthusiasm.

What's in a name?

Leaders introduce young people to many different outdoor activities. Their aims may be educational or recreational or a mixture of both. Educational aims can be linked to formal subject-based learning, physical skills or related to personal and social development. The particular aims will influence the style of leadership, methods of learning and attitudes to the environment.

The table below illustrates five types of outdoor education or recreation and how these elements vary between activities.

Types of outdoor education and leadership

Type of activity	Aims	Environment	Learning	Leader
Outdoor pursuits	Physical skills, new experiences	Gymnasium	Through activities	Instructor
Field studies	Academic, subject-related	Laboratory	Through enquiry, investigation	Teacher, tutor
Development training	Personal and social development	Stage set	Through planning, doing, reviewing	Tutor
Outdoor recreation	Leisure, enjoyment	Park	Through activities	Ranger
Environmental education	More sustainable lifestyles	Home	Awareness, understanding, action	Facilitator

The names given to the leaders of each type of activity can be significant. For example the term 'instructor' used in traditional outdoor pursuits implies the leader is the expert and will impart skills, step by step, to the learner. Instruction suggests a strong level of control over the learning process. The term 'teacher', for most of us, will provoke images of formal learning in schools. It is sometimes used in field studies to make a link between classroom practice and subject-related learning in the outdoors. But field studies, in general, is more likely to be concerned with individual and group needs and leaders referred to as 'tutors', a term which implies more interaction. This term is also used in development training where tutors guide their groups through a learning cycle which includes planning, doing and reviewing. In outdoor recreation there are 'rangers' who offer their groups more informal activities and experiences. The term 'outdoor youth worker' is free of the connotations of control implicit in some of the other terms but its blandness gives no clues to its preferred leadership and learning styles. A term frequently used in environmental education is 'facilitator'. Although this can sound clumsy it does at least make clear the relationship between leader and learner and suggest that the process is about each person being helped to take responsibility for their own learning.

What kind of leader are you?

A leader is best when people barely know he exists, not so good when people obey and acclaim him, worst when they despise him. . . . But of a good leader when his work is done, his aim fulfilled they will say 'We did this ourselves'.

Lao-tse

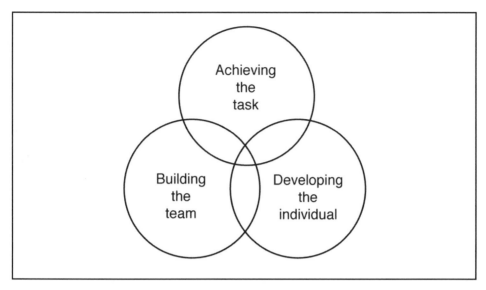

Figure 3.1. Adair's three-circle, action-centred leadership

If you ask a cross-section of the general public, 'What makes a good leader?' you are likely to receive a stereotype of the autocratic, charismatic person who is directed towards achieving a particular goal, such as winning a war, a football trophy or reaching the top of a mountain. If you ask a group of people working in outdoor education the same question you should receive a quite different response. More than likely the qualities they will mention

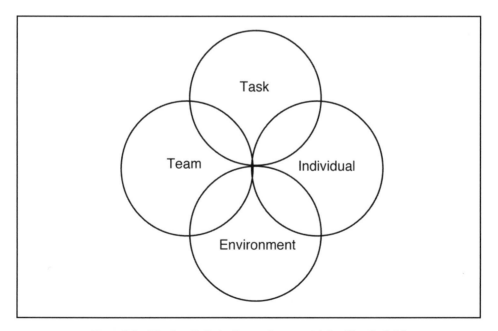

Figure 3.2. The fourth link, the environment (after Ken Ogilvie)

will be: good communication and management, enthusiasm, encourage-
ment, empathy and vision.

John Adair proposed an 'action-centred' model of leadership based on the
interplay of developing the individual, managing the group and achieving
the task (see figure 3.1.).

Ken Ogilvie (1993) in his useful book *Leading and Managing Groups in the
Outdoors* extends this model by considering the importance of the
environment in any decision making. It becomes the fourth circle in the
model (figure 3.2). The effective leader is able to balance the needs of the
individual and group in working towards a common goal and at the same
time maintain a sustainable approach to the environment.

Leadership styles

It is possible to distinguish between two extremes, the 'autocratic' and the
'democratic' styles. An example of the former is the traditional outdoor
instructor or tutor where the leader gives out knowledge and skills and the
task of climbing the mountain, canoeing the rapid or gathering information
takes priority. Compare this with the outdoor leader who acts as a facilitator,
sensitive to the needs of the group and encourages the participants to learn
for themselves. Here the activity or task is of secondary importance. The

implications of these styles is shown in figure 3.3.

In reality the experienced outdoor leader will vary the style according to
the group, situation and environment. As an example, when taking a group
into the mountains for their first overnight camp there will be many
occasions where the leader can share or delegate responsibility. Members of
the group may lead sections of the walk, discussing aspects of route finding
and deciding stopping places amongst themselves. They might choose their
campsite and the particular site for their own tent. Later in the afternoon on
a high level ridge walk the weather changes, there is heavy rain and poor
visibility; the leader's style adapts to the situation. The task of leading the
group safely off the ridge and down to the camp is paramount and the leader
assumes tight control until the group regains safety. Once at the camp, the
group can share responsibility again by preparing the meal.

Leader as Instructor   **Leader as Facilitator**

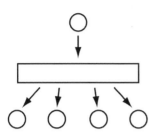 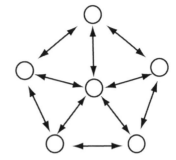

Instructor tells pupils	Leader shares with participants
Teacher dominant	Participatory
Instructing—passing on knowledge and skills	Facilitating—encouraging participants to learn for themselves
Passive	Active
Task oriented	People oriented
Competitive	Co-operative
Environment as gymnasium, laboratory or playground	Environment as home, community or special place
There is one approach to teaching	There are a variety of approaches to learning
Terminology: Instructor, Tutor, Students, Pupils	Terminology: Facilitator, Guide, Learners, Participants
Emphasis on skills, competencies	Emphasis on experience, reflection, learning
Emphasis on equipment as an aid to learning	Emphasis on relationships as an aid to learning

Figure 3.3. Approaches to outdoor learning and leadership

There are many other occasions when an effective, democratic leader may want good control. One example is when the group are journeying through or close to an environmentally sensitive area such as a wetland, ancient woodland or a site used by nesting birds. It might be important to keep the group together, choose the route carefully and travel quietly. Similarly the experienced leader might want a higher level of control when crossing cultivated land, walking through farmyards or passing through a small village. It is essential that the outdoor leader is aware of different leadership styles, knows when a particular style is required and appreciates the effect on their group and their learning.

It is also clear that if we are interested in educating for sustainability then a facilitative, democratic style is most appropriate. There are plenty of equivalents in the outdoors to the classroom teacher who says, 'We are going to learn about democracy today, will you all keep quiet and open your books at page 105'. The media, that is how we do things, must match the message. We probably underestimate the significance of the leader as a role model. Small actions can sometimes speak more than thousands of words (see Chapter 10).

When do we learn best?

An activity which offers leaders useful insights into how we learn is to ask a group to think of the situations when they have learned something quickly. It might be, for instance, learning to ride a bicycle, learning about dinosaurs or learning to be a member of a team.

What were the special ingredients which encouraged them to learn well? I pose this question to many groups and these are the most frequently quoted answers:

- When there is a problem to solve
- When the learning is shared
- When I am involved in doing
- When the learning is related to my life
- When there is a challenge
- When there is time to reflect
- When I enjoy learning

This list is very heartening to those working in outdoor education since good outdoor programmes will include many, if not all, of the above ingredients.

How do we learn?

> I hear and I forget,
> I see and I remember
> I do and I understand.
> Chinese Proverb

Research supports at least part of this old saying. Studies have shown that we retain:

10% of what we read,
20% of what we only hear,
30% of what we only see,
50% of what we see and hear,
70% of what we say as we talk about doing it,
90% of what we say as we do a thing.

These statistics strongly support the value of 'learning by doing' or active learning. They will probably hold no surprises for outdoor leaders but they will confirm the significance of even short periods spent actively in the outdoors.

Experiential learning

Active learning occurs all the time and it is the most natural form of learning. When a leader or facilitator tries to encourage this process and provides a structure for the learning, it is known as experiential learning. This type of learning is holistic, it involves the whole person through feelings, creativity, the physical being as well as the intellect.

John Dewey (1938) was an early proponent of this form of education. He outlined the following basic principles of experiential learning:

- Start with the learner. Consider their knowledge, skills, interests and needs.
- Learning is social and should involve group interaction.
- The learning process is an interaction with the environment.
- Learning needs to engage in problem solving.
- Experience should be reviewed and new learning transferred to future situations.

From these principles it is clear that experiential learning is much more than a haphazard collection of experiences. It is a process of structured learning where individuals respond to and reflect on actual experience and this affects their future decisions. From similar ideas David Kolb (1984) developed his experiential learning cycle. This is adapted into a simple Plan, Do, Review model shown in figure 3.4.

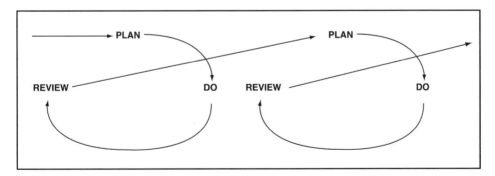

Figure 3.4. Experiential learning

Many outdoor leaders will be familiar with this model as it forms the basis of development training and team building using the outdoors. It has several advantages over traditional forms of teaching where the leader is seen as the font of knowledge:

- It motivates the learner. People enjoy active learning.
- It uses co-operative learning, there is a sharing of knowledge and experience.
- It benefits from different learning styles.
- Learning can be transferred from one situation to another.
- It is democratic and empowers people to take responsibilty for their own learning.

Co-operation and competition in the outdoors

It is important that outdoor leaders are aware of the distinctions between outdoor sport, outdoor recreation and outdoor education. The approaches are quite different even though they may involve the same activity. For example, orienteering as a sport is highly competitive, the aim is for the competitor to achieve the fastest time or the greatest number of points from an event. Orienteering can also be offered as a form of recreation. It is an enjoyable way of exploring an area and getting exercise and fresh air. Many country and forest parks provide orienteering courses to attract visitors to their sites.

Orienteering as part of an outdoor education programme is likely to have different aims. It is an excellent activity to encourage young people to co-operate, make decisions and take responsibility. When leaders are introducing and organising this activity they need to be clear what they are trying to achieve. If they are trying to encourage co-operation or environmental awareness through the activity, it may be counter-productive to emphasise speed and record the time taken to complete the course. In fact the very use of terms such as 'course', 'event', 'start' and 'finish' may be inappropriate. Instead it might be presented more in terms of a 'journey' where small groups are involved in 'way-finding'. There may be other occasions when the aims are different, for example when the outdoor leader wants to introduce young people to the sport, sharpen map reading skills or encourage quick decisions. In these cases, competition may be appropriate. The important point is that the leader is aware of the aims, the choices available and appreciates the potential for gaining different skills and experiences.

Learning in many schools is still based on individualistic and competitive methods. In fact, recent government thinking has favoured these approaches and argued that higher standards in terms of better examination results will follow. Research has shown that individualistic learning methods are successful when the aim is to learn specific information or skills. Competitive approaches are preferable when the aim is to reinforce, review or practise simple factual material using drill or rote methods. However, for a range of higher order skills including thinking creatively, problem solving and applying information to new situations then co-operative learning is more effective. This type of learning also has the benefit of promoting many personal and social skills and more positive attitudes to learning.

Co-operative learning is an essential strategy in educating for change and encouraging more sustainable lifestyles. Outdoor leaders have many opportunities to use co-operative methods in their work and if schools are returning to more traditional, individual and competitive learning it may be even more important that we develop these approaches.

Learning styles

Young people have different learning styles and it is important that outdoor leaders use a variety of teaching methods to meet individual's requirements. There are many theories about learning. Some emphasise the difference between the way we perceive information either in an abstract way through reason or in a concrete way through our physical senses. Anthony Gregorc also believes that once we receive the information there is a preference for the way we arrange it in our minds. Some people prefer to do this in a methodical or sequential way and others do it randomly. This results in four distinct learning styles: concrete sequential, abstract sequential, abstract random and concrete random (see figure 3.5). Each style of learner will have their own preferred activities. For example, the concrete sequential learner will enjoy undertaking scientific fieldwork which involves observing, recording and analysing. The abstract random learner, will prefer group work, discussion and role play where there is a chance to express feelings whilst the concrete random learner may show a particular aptitude at problem solving.

In the 1970s the psychologist, Ornstein, distinguished two modes of thinking, analytical and aesthetic, and related these to separate parts of the brain. He argued that the left hemisphere of the brain is the source of analytical thinking concerned with logical and deductive processes such as mathematics, science and language and the right hemisphere is the seat of our aesthetic or creative thought. Our education system emphasises the importance of left-brain thinking and undervalues learning through our feelings and intuition. As a result, young people who are predominantly right-brain thinkers may underachieve at school. There may be other repercussions for environmental education because analytical thinking tries to make us objective and detached from the world around us. In contrast, it can be argued that right-brain thinking may help to promote connections and empathy towards nature. It is important that both modes of thinking are encouraged and outdoor education can provide many opportunities for aesthetic learning. Some activities, such as route planning and fieldwork involve mainly analytical thinking, whereas many others, such as problem solving, movement, balance and role play are related to more intuitive and creative thinking. In this way, outdoor leaders may help to compensate for an education system based largely on one mode of learning.

Another theory of learning has been proposed by Howard Gardner (1983) who suggests that people have multiple forms of intelligence. He distinguishes seven types of intelligence and argues that teaching in our schools emphasises just two of these, logical-mathematical and linguistic

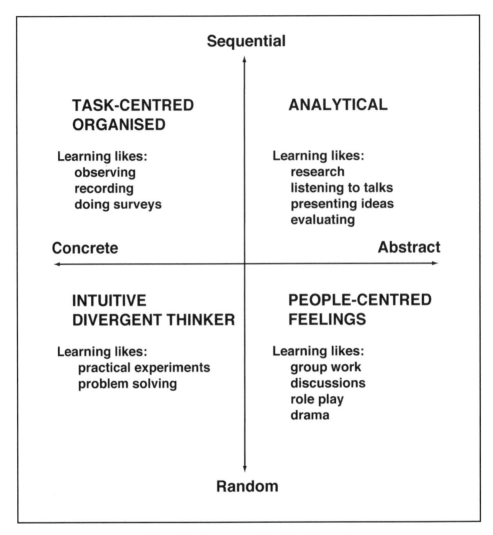

Figure 3.5. Learning styles (after Gregorc)

intelligences. There are other forms such as musical or spatial intelligence, as well as the interpersonal intelligence that recognises how to understand other people and the intrapersonal intelligence of self understanding that are all poorly developed in formal education. It is clear that outdoor leaders can offer many opportunities for young people to develop these other intelligences.

So what does all this theory suggest to us as leaders? I think there are two key points:

1. We should be aware of different learning styles and intelligences within our groups. As far as possible we should try to vary our teaching style and methods to meet these needs.

2. We should be aware that we can compensate for narrow approaches to learning and that for some young people this may represent a dramatic change in their motivation, behaviour or performance. On many occasions, teachers who know young people well in the classroom are surprised by their achievement in outdoor activities. In some cases this represents an unlocking of talent which has not occurred through formal education (see Chapter 2).

As a means of summarising, I can suggest the following short list of guidelines:

Guidelines for the environmental leader

1. *Be aware of your group*
   What is their ability, previous experience?
   What are their expectations?
   What are their preferred learning styles?
   How can you relate to their needs?
2. *Choose appropriate teaching methods*
   Know your aims.
   Be aware of leadership styles.
   Choose your teaching strategy.
3. *Listen and learn*
   Good leadership means good communication.
   Show an interest in and learn from others.
   It is not necessary for you to be the expert in everything.
4. *Show enthusiasm and a sense of wonder*
   Your interest and enthusiasm can inspire.
   Keep a sense of wonder for the environment.
5. *Emphasise sharing and doing*
   Involve the group in active learning rather than telling and showing.
6. *Challenge the group*
   With open questions that challenge their attitudes.
   By encouraging them to use all their senses.
   By providing an adventure.
7. *Make it special*
   Maintain an element of surprise.
   Use stories, analogies, song, poetry to convey messages.
8. *Demonstrate through your own good practice*
   Your actions may speak louder than words.
9. *Encourage confidence and motivation*
   Provide rich, positive experiences.
   Encourage people to repeat similar experiences themselves.
10. *Encourage reflection*
    Reflect on experience.
    Apply learning to new situations.

4. Linking to schools and the community

Why do we need to know about schools?

There have been enormous changes to schools and their curricula over the last ten years. As outdoor leaders who are interested in environmental education it is important to understand these changes for two reasons.

1. We might want to link our outdoor work more closely to the school curriculum and by doing this attract more school groups into the outdoors.
2. We might want to compensate for aspects of education no longer being met through the school curriculum.

Quite likely it will be a combination of these two reasons.

Changes to schools

The establishment of a National Curriculum for schools in England and Wales is only one of a number of changes affecting the organisation and management of schools. Schools are now less tied to local education authorities. They have their own budgets and operate virtually as small businesses. Some schools have become completely independent of the local authority and have adopted grant maintained status. The role of the school governing bodies has changed, they are now more involved in decision making and the influence of parents has increased. The National Curriculum has brought with it testing at the end of four key stages, at 7, 11, 14 and 16 years of age. League tables are published to compare schools' results and each school has a regular inspection and report on its progress.

These wide reaching changes were imposed by the Conservative Government of the 1980s on a teaching profession which was largely reluctant to change. It represented a cultural shift from the child-centred, progressive education of the 1960s and 1970s to a more teacher-dominant, knowledge-based model. The new Labour Government of 1997 appears to be maintaining this policy. As a result the language of education has changed (see figure 4.1).

The new language is one of control. It is the language of centralisation and of business. It is a far cry from our aims in outdoor and environmental education. It is the language of order, where the aim is to conform to the system rather than an education designed to encourage choice and to change the system (see figure 4.2). Ironically, many other European countries, including most east European countries, are moving towards a more

Business oriented		Student oriented	
Accountability	Inspection	Attitudes	Feelings
Achievement	League table	Celebration	Imagination
Appraisal	Management	Co-operation	Inspiration
Assessment	Performance	Creativity	Needs
Attainment	Testing	Curiosity	Support
Competition	Value for money	Enjoyment	Values
Information		Experience	Wonder

Figure 4.1. Two languages of education

child-centred, participatory model at a time when we are moving in the other direction.

National Curriculum and whole-school curriculum

The Education Reform Act of 1988 established a National Curriculum in England and Wales. This includes ten foundation subjects (English, maths, science, technology, history, geography, art, music, PE and a modern language) which must be taught according to particular programmes of study. It does not include environmental education which was considered as one of five cross-curricular themes that would be taught indirectly through the foundation subjects. This was not a statutory requirement and when the content of the National Curriculum was slimmed down in the first review in 1994 the cross-curricular themes all but disappeared.

There is, however, some scope to teach environmental education in this formal curriculum. A glance at the revised Orders for each subject will show the potential. Let us take an example of a 13 year old student who will be taking all ten foundation subjects at Key Stage 3. What environmental education can she expect? The following summary below shows possibilities from four subjects.

Figure 4.2. Models of education

Goal	Teaching/learning styles	Approach	Outcomes
Education for work	Autocratic: teacher dominated Passive learning Individual responsibility Individual achievement	Content based	To fit the system
Education for life	Participatory: child centred Active learning Shared responsibility Co-operation encouraged	Content and process based	To make choices, to change the system

Geography

Nine geographical themes are investigated. One of these is *Environmental Issues* in which students are taught:

- why some areas are viewed as being of great scenic attraction, and how conflicting demands on the areas can arise
- how attempts are made to plan and manage such environments and how they can have unintended effects
- how considerations of sustainable development, trusteeship and conservation affect environmental planning and management
- about the provision of a reliable supply of fresh water and the causes, effects and prevention of water pollution
- about provision of a reliable supply of energy and the effect on the environment of the development of two different energy sources.

There are other themes such as *Weather and climate* and *Development* which include concepts relevant to environmental education such as 'the water cycle', 'quality of life' and 'the interdependence of countries'.

Science

The two attainment targets of particular relevance are *Life processes* and *Living things and physical processes*. The former considers concepts such as habitats, food chains, pyramids of numbers, food webs and the impact of toxic materials on food chains. The latter considers the variety of energy resources, renewable and non-renewable resources, and the transfer and conservation of energy.

Physical education

Within the general requirements for PE there is an important reference to the development of positive attitudes to others and the environment.

Design and technology

There are important references to the environment in the sections on the evaluation of the quality of products. Students are asked to consider the impact of manufacture and use on the environment.

Although these foundation subjects do offer possibilities for introducing environmental education they do not provide a programme of study. They concentrate on knowledge, learning about the environment rather than the attitudes and values necessary to change behaviour. The learning may be haphazard as the information will come from different subject teachers. There will not necessarily be an environmental education co-ordinator to put the pieces together and to develop an appropriate process for learning.

In Scotland, environmental education has a more central place in the proposed 5–14 curriculum which is divided into five areas: mathematics, English language, expressive arts, religious and moral education and environmental studies. The framework for the latter consists of science, social subjects, technology, health education and information technology. Although much of the content of environmental studies is knowledge and skills based, it also aims to 'develop informed attitudes and values relating to the care and conservation of the environment'.

Fortunately school life and experiences are more than the sum of the National Curriculum subjects. There is a much broader concept called the whole-school curriculum, which can be thought of as everything that goes on in a school that results in students learning about the world around them. This curriculum can include:

- the National Curriculum
- cross-curricular themes and skills
- school assemblies
- special events
- field studies and outdoor education
- environmental action in the school
- extracurricular activities, for example award schemes and clubs
- community, national and international links
- the 'hidden' curriculum: the ethos of the school, the fabric of the buildings, the school grounds, the management and inter personal relations.

This is shown in figure 4.3.

Spiritual, moral, social and cultural considerations

Perhaps the greatest potential to encourage more sustainable action inside and outside of school is through spiritual, moral, social and cultural considerations. The Education Reform Act of 1993 states that:

> The curriculum of a school satisfies the requirements of the Act if it is a balanced and broadly based curriculum which:
> (a) promotes the spiritual, moral, cultural, mental and physical development of pupils at the school and of society; and
> (b) prepares such pupils for the opportunities, responsibilities and experiences of adult life.

As a result of this act, school inspectors are asked to evaluate and report on each school's provision for its pupils' spiritual, moral, social and cultural development. It is helpful to consider the differences between these elements of personal and social development.

Spiritual development
This refers to the opportunities young people are given to reflect on their personal existence and to consider the importance of non-material values in their lives. 'Spiritual' is not synonomous with 'religious' and all areas of the curriculum can contribute to spiritual development.

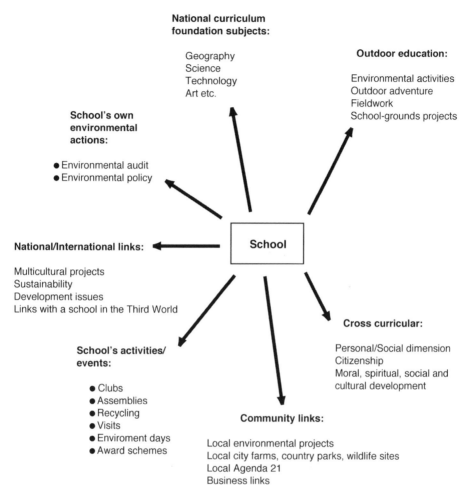

**National curriculum
foundation subjects:**

Geography
Science
Technology
Art etc.

Outdoor education:

Environmental activities
Outdoor adventure
Fieldwork
School-grounds projects

**School's own
environmental
actions:**

- Environmental audit
- Environmental policy

National/International links:

Multicultural projects
Sustainability
Development issues
Links with a school in the Third World

School

Cross curricular:

Personal/Social dimension
Citizenship
Moral, spiritual, social and
cultural development

**School's activities/
events:**

- Clubs
- Assemblies
- Recycling
- Visits
- Enviroment days
- Award schemes

Community links:

Local environmental projects
Local city farms, country parks, wildlife sites
Local Agenda 21
Business links

Figure 4.3. Whole-school approach to environmental education

Moral development

This refers to a young person's knowledge, understanding and behaviour in relation to right and wrong. It is about respect for other people and other life, about truth and justice.

Social development

This refers to how well young people relate to others in different social settings, take responsibility, show initiative, work together in groups and participate co-operatively in school and the wider community. It is about playing an active and responsible role in society.

Cultural development

This refers to young people's understanding and appreciation of aspects of their own and other cultures.

Many of these aspects of personal and social development will be encouraged through subjects in the formal school curriculum. The day-to-day life of the school, its ethos, management, teaching and learning styles etc. will also be influential. However, the importance of links with the wider community and real life experiences in the outdoors cannot be underestimated. Outdoor leaders may play a key role in promoting these elements of personal and social development for young people. Many examples of how leaders can encourage social skills through their outdoor programmes and activities have been given in earlier chapters. Here are a two examples which relate to spiritual, moral and cultural awareness.

Inspiration through environmental experience

Simple travel on foot, by canoe, by sail or by bicycle can bring us into close contact with the environment. If the aim is speed, competition or information gathering we are un-likely to connect with the world around us. If the aim is to explore and we are open to chance happenings and diversions, our awareness is magnified. The wonder and beauty of nature is all around. Some

Simple travel can bring us closer to nature.

landscapes and situations, such as a sunset in the mountains or a clear night sky at sea, have great potential to inspire young people. Outdoor leaders can sometimes plan for these experiences through, for example night walks and bivvies, although the weather will often provide an element of uncertainty. But we do not always need the spectacular, the dramatic landscapes and scenes of grandeur to encourage a sense of wonder. Leaders can encourage young people to explore the more immediate world of nature—the bark of a tree, lichen on a gravestone, reflections on a pond, a spider's web. Exposure to the intricate beauty of life can uplift the spirits, give simple pleasure and call into question our value systems. These experiences can transcend self-centred and material-istic values and help us to appreciate that we form a small part of a greater whole.

Some ideas to help leaders to encourage spiritual development through environmental experiences are given in Chapter 5.

Cultural traditions, moral dilemmas, real life environmental issues

Outdoor experiences provide great scope for discussing our cultural heritage. Through interpreting landscapes we appreciate the influence of nature and the long history of people living in and working the landscape. In Britain there are few completely natural areas and many landscapes have been shaped by people from prehistoric times. Forest cover has been removed over centuries for timber, fuel and to provide grazing for animals. These managed landscapes are a celebrated part of our culture.

But behind the picture-postcard view of our countryside are many social, economic and political issues which affect the environment.

As an example, we can consider the situation in some of our National Parks which include upland landscapes maintained for sheep farming by economic subsidies. This system supports the farming communities and conserves the traditional features of the landscape, such as field barns and drystone walls. It may also help to attract thousands of visitors to the area. Unfortunately it has also led to over-grazing, the spread of acid grassland and the loss of habitats and reduced the diversity of plant and animal species. Thus current policies which benefit local traditions may be harmful to the environment.

There are other issues which may provoke stronger moral feelings. Fox hunting is a cultural tradition in many parts of Britain and some farmers would argue that it is the most effective way to control this predator. Other people would argue that this activity is morally unacceptable if we are concerned with protecting wild species. But consider the question of the red and the grey squirrel. Should the grey be selectively killed to protect the indigenous red? Should some species gain extra protection because of their rarity or because they appeal for cultural reasons? These are moral dilemmas which face the whole society. They are issues that jolt our value system. There are many such issues that can be presented more effectively to groups experiencing the environment directly.

Government action on environmental education

The Conservative Government produced a leaflet at the end of 1996 proclaiming a 'Government Strategy for Environmental Education in England'. The leaflet stated:

> Environmental education is a central means of furthering the Government's commitment to sustainable development. It gives people that capacity to address environmental issues which is vital to achieving a sustainable society. Education in its broadest sense includes personal awareness, experience and interests developed over a period of time—whether at home, at school, college or university, at work, or in the wider community—as well as more formal study.

Although the strategy to achieve this was not made clear, this was at least a statement of support for environmental education.

Much more progress has been made in Scotland with an excellent report, 'Learning for Life' produced in1993 and proposing a national strategy for environmental education. This became the basis for the 'Scottish Strategy for Environmental Education', a statement of intent by the Secretary of State for Scotland in 1995. This report recognises the potential of outdoor education to contribute to environmental education and the need for leisure and recreation organisations to draw up codes of good environmental practice.

Soon after taking office in 1997 the Labour Government committed itself to 'continue to encourage environmental education, inside and out of school'. There was no reference to environmental education in the subsequent White Paper, 'Excellence in Schools'. This did, however, recognise the importance of promoting citizenship in schools partly in response to the level of apathy and cynicism towards politicians and public life. Citizenship, like environmental education, was one of the original cross-curricular themes but its teaching has been piecemeal. A special cross-party committee which will report in 1998 is likely to recommend the inclusion of citizenship in the revised national curriculum for 2000. It is seen as a way of helping young people to understand the political process, appreciate their rights and responsibilities and to participate in their own communities. If these are the outcomes it is clearly good for the democratic process and would support a more sustainable society. Citizenship will also help to encourage the growing links between schools and their communities.

Youth, community and environment

Most outdoor leaders are not involved with formal education but work with youth and community groups in the informal sector. Their work may be with voluntary or local authority agencies and will be broadly concerned with providing social, educational and recreational opportunities. In the youth sector there is no agreed curriculum but at a Ministerial Conference held in 1990 it was accepted that the purpose of youth work should be to offer young people opportunities which are:

- educative—enabling young people to gain necessary skills, knowledge and attitudes
- designed to promote equality of opportunity
- participative—so that they become partners in the learning process and in decision making
- empowering—supporting them to understand and act on the personal, social and political issues which affect their lives

This democratic framework provides a sound basis for education for sustainability. It is further supported by the learning methods which are common to both youth and community work. Whereas in formal education the teacher is responsible for imparting a body of knowledge, in the informal sector an experiential model can be adopted with the leader acting as a facilitator addressing the concerns and interests of the group. The learning is by active involvement in real issues. What is missing is a focus for this work. Local Agenda 21s can provide such a focus and at the same time encourage more sustainable lifestyles.

What is Local Agenda 21?

An agenda is a list of actions that have to be undertaken to achieve certain goals. Local Agenda 21 is an attempt to get people working together to create better environments and a better quality of life. The idea came from the United Nations' Earth Summit in Rio in 1992 when the world's leaders drew up an 'Agenda 21', a programme of action for the 21st century. It was thought the best way to achieve this was by individuals and communities taking their own action at a local level. So Local Agenda 21s are being designed to address common concerns and encourage more sustainable living in terms of housing, environment, transport, health care and social life. They are a way to plan for the future so that we can maintain a good quality of life for our children.

How does a Local Agenda 21 happen? In some places communities are working to establish their own agendas and getting support from their local authorities to carry through their ideas. In other places local authorities are helping to co-ordinate forums on local issues and are encouraging people to work together to improve their environment. In all cases, Local Agenda 21s are partnerships which may include local groups, schools, businesses, environmental agencies and local authorities.

Local Agenda 21 involves:

- knowing what we value in our own environment and deciding how we can protect it
- considering how our actions affect other places and people, in our community, in our country and in other parts of the planet
- thinking in much longer timescales, beyond our own lifetimes
- finding a fairer basis to share resources
- meeting others to exchange ideas, agree common goals and draw up an agenda for action
- working together to create a healthy and sustainable environment

---

How can outdoor leaders contribute to Local Agenda 21?

1. *By encouraging environmental awareness.* Outdoor leaders can encourage young people to appreciate the special qualities of a particular environment.
2. *Through motivation and confidence.* Success in the outdoors leads to motivated and confident young people who are more likely to get involved in local action.
3. *By encouraging personal and social skills.* Through group work and team-building, outdoor leaders can encourage co-operation, thinking and communication skills.
4. *By emphasising the importance of the quality of life.* The outdoors can provide opportunities to enjoy the simpler pleasures of fresh air, natural beauty and wildlife.
5. *By acting as a role model for young people.* Through your own good practice.

Practice

5. Encouraging a personal response to the environment

We are of the earth; our flesh is grass. We live in the cycle of birth and death, growth and decay. Our bodies respond to daily rhythms of light and darkness, to the tug of the moon, and to the change of seasons. The salt content of our blood, our genetic similarity to other life forms, and our behaviour at every turn gives us away. We are shot through with wildness. . . . we are of the earth. We have an affinity for nature. What do we do about that simple but overwhelming fact?

David Orr (1994)

Introduction

When did you last smell the earth; touch the bark of a tree; look really closely at some lichen growing on a wall; stand or sit and absorb the sights, sounds and smells of a quiet place?

The vast majority of people in Western societies do not feel connected to the earth. Our lives separate us from nature. We try to hide the 'wildness' described above by David Orr. Yet the re-awakening of our senses and the reconnection to nature could be the key to changing attitudes and behaviour. Greater knowledge of ecology and environmental issues has not always led to greater awareness and action for the environment. Studies in countries as culturally diverse as Hungary and Japan have shown that scientific knowledge of the environment has not produced changes in attitudes and behaviour (Victor Andras, 1991). Rather, we need to touch the hearts of people and encourage them to forge a personal link with the earth. The author John Fowles argues, 'we know quite enough facts now; what we are still miserably retarded in is in our emotional and aesthetic relationship. . . . An intense need and affection for the direct experience of nature . . . is the only kind of soil in which a really effective social demand for conservation can grow.'

Unplug the computer, tune in to the environment

We live in a world of increasing technology and our knowledge comes from secondary sources such as television, the Internet and CD-Roms. From these sources we have a more and more detailed scientific knowledge of our environment. We may appreciate the problems but still not make the connections with our own lives.

Some people believe the computer and its access to unlimited information is the key to understanding environmental issues and helping society to manage them. They argue that computers are more efficient than the human mind, they can analyse masses of data, run simulation exercises and suggest courses of action. They allow us increased objectivity. But do they help us live more sustainable lives?

It is easy to get seduced by modern information technology, it offers us precise answers at the push of a button. But it may also help to divorce us from the natural world. It is essential that we have direct contact with our environment, that we engage with issues on the ground, that we use our feelings and intuition. Computers do not allow us to do this. Images and information displayed on a TV screen or computer monitor may present a false impression of the real situation. Chet Bowers (1990) argues that 'the com-

puter is useful in helping us to understand the nature and complexity of ecological disruption, but it is of little use in coming to grips with the culturally embedded pattern of consciousness that causes us to act as though we are not an interdependent part of the biotic community'.

Computers are useful tools and can help us gain knowledge about complex systems. But they cannot give us the answers. We need to appreciate our connections with the earth. How we understand our moral relationship with the rest of the biotic community is more essential to our long-term survival.

I believe the technological age has made the work of outdoor leaders in providing real experiences for young people even more vital. So let us unplug the computer and tune in to the environment. This section offers ideas on how leaders can start this process by providing young people with direct experiences of nature.

Sensory activities

Young children have a natural curiosity about their environment and enjoy learning through direct experience. As we grow older we insulate ourselves from nature through material possessions, cars, central heating, indoor entertainment. We become viewers rather than participants. I remember visiting the Grand Canyon, one of the world's most stunning landscapes, and being surprised to find more people inside the little visitor centre on the rim of the canyon looking through the window at the scene than those outside in the morning air. We see a similar phenomenon in the popularity of cruising holidays, where passengers travel in a capsule of comfort and convenience from island to island with minimum contact with local people or the environment. Today we can move from home to car to shopping precinct and entertainment centre without ever confronting the vagaries of our weather. The new generation may never know what it is like to get soaked to the skin or be buffeted by the wind.

As outdoor leaders we can challenge this culture and help young people to rebuild personal connections. But there is a need to be sensitive in our approach. Many young people will have barriers to making direct contact with the earth. Here are a few considerations:

- Teenagers are likely to be influenced by peer pressure. It may not be 'cool' to get close to the earth.
- They may not wish to get 'dirty' or spoil their clothes.
- They may feel self-conscious about doing something different or behaving in a way which, to them, may appear childlike.

The leader needs to set the scene, choose activities carefully for the group, encourage support, trust and co-operation and let nature play its part.

There is a wide variety of materials available to leaders. Sensory activities have been used for many years particularly in the United States where they were developed by Steve van Matre (1972) and through the education and interpretation programmes of the US National Parks. Ideas have also been introduced to Britain through the books of Joseph Cornell (1979, 1989) and Thom Henley (1989). These activities have become increasingly popular with rangers wishing to introduce young people to country parks and urban wildlife sites. They have spread to many other groups using the outdoors.

I include a few examples of activities designed to encourage sensory awareness:

Activity—Blindfold walk

Young people work in pairs. One is blindfolded and led carefully and in silence by the 'guide' on a short walk. The guide helps their partner to explore nature by senses other than sight. The partner may be guided to crawl through a bush, climb over a fallen branch, smell some fungi, touch a berry, sit and listen to the wind or running water. The walk is short, it may be only 50 metres long, but it may include walking uphill and downhill, on dry ground and through wet areas and the guide should choose stopping places to encourage sensory awareness. After about 10 minutes the guide leads their partner back to the start and removes the blindfold. The partner then tries to retrace the route stopping here and there to repeat the touches, sounds or smells. It is unusual for the person to discover the exact route or even remember what happened at each stopping place, so prompting is necessary and there will be surprises in store. Partners then change roles and the new guide chooses a different route with plenty of sensory activities on the way.

This activity is popular with all age groups. It involves a lot of trust and it is important that once blindfolded the young person is led with care, particularly when approaching trees and branches.

Activity—Viewfinders

This activity encourages young people to focus on details in the environment. The first stage is to make some simple viewfinders from natural materials. The viewfinder will be a small rectangular frame, about 6 cm × 4 cm. It can be made by splitting and threading grass or reeds or weaving a few small twigs together. Get the participants to view the environment through their view-finders from different angles. Use the frame to capture landscape and portrait views. Lie on the ground and frame a cloud or the canopy of a tree, get a good vantage point for a distant view and choose your favourite close-up which may be an insect, a flower or a dewdrop. Let a partner see the ones you like best and share their favourite views.

The activity can be extended by working in pairs taking turns to be the 'photographer' and the 'camera'. The camera, with eyes closed, is led to the place where the photographer wishes to take the picture and is carefully positioned for the photo. The photographer gently turns the earlobe of the camera which acts as a shutter, the camera's eyes are opened for just one second to make the exposure. Three photos are taken, and later discussed before changing places. Try to encourage unusual close-up shots, with care the camera can be moved close to the ground.

Activity—Touch hunt

This is a scavenger hunt with a difference. Participants are asked to search for and collect half a dozen natural 'touches'. The list should encourage young people to pick up and feel natural objects and to choose which best fits the description. A few examples are: something *crunchy*, something *bendy*, something *rough*, something *sticky*, something *tickly*, something *cold*.

This is a good activity for individuals to join together in small groups of four or five to share their 'touches' and to decide which six objects of all those collected they will select for their 'exhibition of touches' which will be open to visitors from the other groups.

Activity—Down to earth

This is an activity which helps to get rid of inhibitions about touching the ground, the grass, dead leaves and the soil. The best location is a woodland area with lots of dry decaying leaves. Participants remove shoes and socks and lie on the ground. Each person's body is covered with leaves, twigs, pine needles or grass until just the face is clear. They are asked to use their senses to experience this insect's view of the world. Young people are usually happy to spend ten or fifteen minutes on this activity. Give a signal when it is time to emerge from their blankets. It can be used as a 'stilling' experience at the end of an active day. It is also a good position to view the starry sky on a clear night. This is an unusual experience and young people will be keen to share their feelings.

Activity—Special places

This is a more structured activity, participants are given a little card with a small number of activities to do in a 'special place'. They are asked to choose their own place to sit for about 20 minutes. They should spend some time choosing their place so they feel comfortable and relaxed, it should be special to them for some reason. With some groups it may help for each person to be in sight of at least one other participant. An example of activities to do in their special place is shown in figure 5.1.

Young people often enjoy sharing their experiences after time at their special places. Some may wish to read their haiku to the rest of the group but others may prefer to keep their thoughts and feelings to themselves.

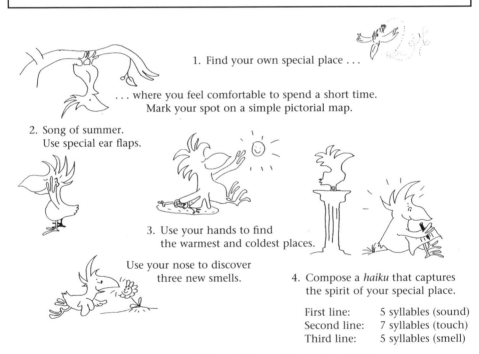

1. Find your own special place . . .

. . . where you feel comfortable to spend a short time. Mark your spot on a simple pictorial map.

2. Song of summer. Use special ear flaps.

3. Use your hands to find the warmest and coldest places.

Use your nose to discover three new smells.

4. Compose a *haiku* that captures the spirit of your special place.

First line: 5 syllables (sound)
Second line: 7 syllables (touch)
Third line: 5 syllables (smell)

Figure 5.1.   Special places (illustrated by Andrea Déri)

Sensory activities such as those described can be put together as part of a journey. Van Matre (1974) describes how sensory activities can be carefully selected so that they flow from one to another as part of a 'quiet walk' or 'earthwalk'. These activities can also be used by leaders to build a personal relationship with a small environment before introducing a piece of fieldwork. They may also be an appropriate way of encouraging sensitivity and reflection after an energetic day of group activity.

Time alone in nature

Many traditional societies throughout the world have recognised the value of solitude to encourage reflection and personal growth. Sometimes young people spent time alone travelling as part of a 'rite of passage', the transition from one stage of life to another particularly from youth to adulthood. Young Aboriginal males in Australia undertook a 'walkabout', whereas Plains Indian adolescent boys went out into the wilderness alone as part of a 'vision quest', enduring hardship and seeking a vision from their animal spirits. Solitude was seen as a way of developing self awareness and independence and allowing young people to gain deep insights into life and their role in society.

Adventure programmes, such as those developed by Outward Bound, have for many years promoted the benefits of solo experiences for personal development. Few current outdoor programmes can justify allowing time for a 24-hour solo but there are still opportunities for short periods of time alone in nature. These solos may be key experiences in terms of developing feelings for and connections with nature. In fact, I would go further and suggest that there is an inner need to relate to other forms of life in this way. How else do you explain the popularity of fishing in urban areas across Britain? The solitary anglers seen daily, in all weathers, fishing in ponds and along canal banks are not just there for the catch. They are demonstrating the need to get away from the trappings and noise of everyday life as much as the lone sailor or single person tramping the fells.

I am often surprised at how much enjoyment young people gain from solitude in a natural setting. Frequently they will ask to return to the special place where they first experienced time by themselves. These experiences are probably more powerful when there is no structure or task, such as writing up a log or a diary. Nothing to make us analyse or sequence our thoughts. Thoughts can then flow freely, the senses are awakened to sounds and smells, the eyes may focus on a tiny insect or capture shapes in the clouds overhead. Such experiences can help us to appreciate the interconnectedness of life and may lead to a spiritual awareness.

Adventure and sensory awareness

There is great scope to encourage sensory awareness through adventurous activities in the outdoors. Harold Drasdo (1972), in a classic essay on outdoor education, stresses the connections between adventure and visual awareness. He illustrates this by considering the climber:

> his eye moves freely between what is general and what is local, at one moment ranging over the entire landscape to the horizon, at the next working back to the cliff structure, the setting of the pitch upon it and the progress of the other climber on the pitch; in the second phase the eye moves between the local and the particular, from the line of the pitch to an inspection of minute finger and toe holds. This span of visual awareness, continued through a period of hours in

regular sequences of concentration and relaxation, extending from the small detail to the entire vista, must be nearly unique in human activity.

It is common for the adventurer's awareness to be heightened through intense concentration. The climber gets to know the intimate nature of the rock whilst moving across its surface. The canoeist becomes part of the flow of the water, reading its rapids and eddies. The sailor senses slight changes in the wind and adjusts boat, body and sail. They feel nature directly, their understanding is through all their senses.

Dramatic scenery can raise our awareness. Alone or in small groups in wild areas, on the sea, in mountains, canyons or deserts, we are often humbled, our own life may be put into perspective, we begin to feel connected. Walking alone across a desert for the first time in Big Bend National Park in Texas, I was aware of intense smells, the almost imperceptible sound of a snake as it slid across the earth, the exquisite beauty of a solitary crimson flower and the struggle for life of the living rock cactus. It would be difficult not to be moved by such an experience.

This might be seen as esoteric, not many young people get the opportunity to experience the desert but many are introduced to relatively wild areas and frequently want to express their feelings:

> It's hard to put this down on paper, all the feelings during the expedition to the mountains. The feeling of being so close to nature and its hidden mysteries, so close to the harmony composed by the birds' songs was unforgettable. . . . So tired but so pleased to have the opportunity to touch, to feel, to smell, to walk for 5 or 6 hours through the mountains. . . . So cold during the night but so warm with the others around, watching the shooting stars and making wishes for the future. . . . So insecure of falling down the rocks but so secure that nature won't leave us helpless. . . . So many things to observe but so little time.

Spiritual awareness

There are many examples, similar to the one above, of leaders and young people having deep experiences in the outdoors. The American psychologist, Abraham Maslow called these 'peak experiences', when there is a feeling of connectedness, a heightened sense of being alive. These experiences can be very powerful and may provide a turning point in a person's life. They are spiritual experiences. Jean Liedloff (1989) a psychotherapist describes how during a walk alone in some woods in Maine, she was suddenly confronted by a glade:

> the whole picture had a completeness, an all-there quality, of such dense power that it stopped me in my tracks. I went to the edge and then, softly, as though into a magical or holy place, to the centre, where I sat, then lay down with my cheek against the freshness of the moss. It is here, I thought, and I felt the anxiety that coloured my life fall away. . . . I felt I had discovered the missing centre of things, the key to rightness itself, and must hold on to knowledge that was so clear in that place.

The glade was her sacred place and became her metaphor for understanding life. Later she rediscovered her 'glade' in the tropical rain forest of South America.

J. Gary Knowles (1992), a professor of education, describes a similar spiritual experience that changed his life. He was leading a night-time canoe trip across a lake in New Zealand with a group of 15 year olds from the city. He comments on the excitement and apprehension of the group as they set off under a myriad of stars. Suddenly they were faced by an illumination over the lake from thousands of glow worms:

> They were breathtaking. Each tiny glow came from a single phosphorescent light-emitting creature. Suspended like delicate jewels, the larvae of the fungus gnat had emerged to feed, their diffused glow reflecting on the faces of the exuberant students. . . . we listened intently to the night and to each other. I was silent, allowing nature to speak. . . . many students marvelled at the power of beauty and the place's serenity. . . . In my mind, and in the minds of several students, a sacred place was established. It was the site of a special event, a place, if you will, at which individuals united with the powers of nature.

The leader's role

The leader cannot predict or programme such spiritual experiences, they are spontaneous and result from a particular set of circumstances. J. Gary Knowles returned with similar groups to canoe the same lake at night but the intensity of the first experience was never repeated. But I know through experience that direct contact with the natural environment, particularly in challenging situations can be inspirational. In its most powerful form it can lead to feelings of belonging or 'oneness' with the earth. Leaders can set the scene and make use of opportunities as they arise. They can introduce awareness activities which re-awaken our senses and encourage feelings of connectedness.

Peter Higgins (1996) puts forward a strong case for using an 'elemental' approach in outdoor education. He argues that the 'elements' of earth, fire, water, air, weather, shelter, food, darkness and silence are fundamental to our existence. These themes provide many opportunities for young people to express feelings and reconnect with nature. For example, he makes the point that few people experience real darkness in the outdoors. Our cities and suburbs have a continual glow of background light. He says that: 'the night sky has been a source of wonder and inspiration since man evolved a questioning consciousness. Many young people question their place in the universe when exposed to such stimuli.'

This work in outdoor education has the ability to reach the hearts as well as the minds and bodies of young people. It could be even more important than we realise in changing our attitudes and behaviour as a prerequisite for more sustainable ways of life.

6. Personal response through the visual arts and creative writing

> Art is a way of entering the environment attentively, our senses awakened; it enlarges the world and induces a feeling of awe about it.
>
> Andy Goldsworthy

The visual arts

The visual arts can be a very powerful way of introducing young people to the environment. Art can reawaken our senses and help to re-establish personal connections with our environment. It offers a different way of gaining knowledge and can balance the more common scientific approach with an aesthetic approach to understanding. Art can inspire young people who do not respond to the more traditional forms of communication.

There have always been strong links between art and environment. The relationship between artist and environment is complex and is influenced by traditions and culture. The environment can be a stimulus for art and at the same time art can stimulate environmental awareness. Art is a way of making a personal response, an expression of feelings for the environment. Outdoor leaders with just a little experience can help young people enjoy and appreciate art and this may offer them another approach to express their imagination and creativity.

Personal response through the visual arts and creative writing.

Art and environment as inspiration

The environment is a constant source of inspiration to artists and art encourages an awareness and interest in the environment. The first artists, the Palaeolithic cave painters, expressed their relationship with their environment by depicting the animals they hunted. Wildlife scenes of flying fish and dolphins are found on frescoes from the ancient Minoan civilisation of Crete. Chinese painting from early times has celebrated scenery and particularly the wild landscapes of mountain and waterfall. In China the Taoist philosophy was of people living in harmony with nature and landscape painting and poetry was a strong tradition.

European art came from different roots, the Judeo–Christian belief that people had dominion over nature. For hundreds of years art was subordinate to the Church and artists produced biblical scenes. The mediaeval mind feared wild places; mountains and forests were threatening, the homes of thieves and savage beasts. These attitudes gradually changed and the Romantic movement of the nineteenth century began to celebrate dramatic landscapes. J. M. W. Turner and Claude Monet are examples of artists who were inspired by the forces of nature, the power of the wind and rain, storms, clouds and sea. Turner was tied to the mast of a ship to experience the impact of a storm which inspired his *Steamer in a Snowstorm*. Turner's paintings show the insignificance of people in relationship to the uncontrollable power of nature. Monet spent hours experiencing the waves lashing the coast, he painted the storms whilst the salt water spattered him. He was fascinated by elemental subjects, the transient effects of light and atmosphere. His later paintings of dappled light on water help us to see the world afresh. The work of sculptors like Henry Moore and Barbara Hepworth has been inspired by natural forms. It is not difficult to see the links between the weathered gritstone blocks of the Pennine moors and some of Henry Moore's sculptures. For Moore, 'everything in the world of form is understood through our bodies,' a concept which many outdoor leaders can relate to easily.

Through their work these artists help us to see with fresh eyes and we are drawn to detail in nature we may have missed or ignored. This is art communicating meaning, helping us to know and understand not through facts and concepts but through feelings. We begin to appreciate pattern, colour, shape, beauty. We are attracted to the outdoors and appreciate landscapes and wild places through art.

Environmental art

Some environmental artists have extended the idea of a deep personal relationship with the earth. One example is Andy Goldsworthy who works outdoors with natural materials, such as slate, leaves, twigs, snow, sand etc. He believes that a personal relationship with the environment is essential for his art. In fact the two are inseparable:

> When I began working outside I had to establish instincts and feelings for nature—some I never had whilst others I had not used since childhood. I splashed in water, covered myself in mud, went barefoot and woke with the dawn. I needed a physical link before a personal approach and relationship could be formed.
> For me, looking, touching, material, place and form are all inseparable from the resulting work. It is difficult to say where one stops and another begins.

Andy Goldsworthy makes direct contact with nature and experiences materials in much the same way as a climber may get to know the qualities of the rock on which they move.

His work is often transient; a stone archway collapses, icicles melt, leaves are blown away and he records these natural sculptures, or land art, on photographs. It is easy to relate to Andy Goldsworthy's art, it often takes us by surprise and we realise the beauty of the simple natural materials around us. Young people can be easily inspired by photographs of Andy Goldsworthy's work (for examples of his work see Goldsworthy 1990 and 1994). His ideas and approaches can be used as a basis for involving young people in making simple pieces of land art.

Sandi Stevens, an outdoor education teacher based at Low Bank Ground, Coniston has developed ideas for introducing land art to leaders and young people. Her approach is simple and flexible. Leaders who are a little uncertain should go outside for 10 or 15 minutes and try it for themselves. Land art can be used as a short session to encourage environmental awareness at the beginning or end of a day or developed as a half day or full day activity. Here are some guidelines for leaders based on Sandi's work:

Guidelines for leading a land art session

Why do land art?
Land art is a method of encouraging young people to explore the environment by choosing and using natural materials to create a piece of art in the outdoors. It awakens our senses and helps us to

become aware of the diversity and beauty of the natural world. Young people are encouraged to make a personal response and to reflect on their own and other people's work. Land art does not make the same demands as drawing or painting and most young people are motivated by the activity.

How to lead a land art session
You do not need to be an artist to lead a land art session. Here are some ideas on organising the activity:

1. Give a short introduction to art and the environment. Explain what you are trying to achieve. To inspire your group, show photographs of the work of some artists who use the outdoors. Try not to concentrate on just one artist or show too many examples as this can lead to imitating the artist's work rather than producing fresh ideas. You could also show the group a simple piece of land art you have produced.
2. Choose an area with plenty of natural materials and where there will be little disturbance from other people. Avoid sensitive, wildlife areas such as nature reserves as the activity involves a certain amount of collecting and some trampling. Examples of suitable areas are a wood, an old quarry, a seashore or even waste ground.
3. Describe the boundaries of your area. Encourage individuals to walk around to get the feel and mood of the place. Ask them to use their senses, to look closely, to touch, to smell, to walk bare foot, to lie down. Let them examine leaves, mosses, flowers, seed heads, berries, bark, twigs, branches, mud, sand, stone etc. and to consider their colour, tone, texture, shape and weight.
4. Ask them to select carefully and use natural materials around them to create a sculpture, pattern or design. Emphasise a gentle approach, it is not necessary to uproot or damage plants. The materials can be fixed together by gluing with spit, weaving with grass or branches, pinning with thorns or through leaning, suspending or balancing. Simple ideas often give the most effective results.
5. Their choice of site is important, as their work can become part of the landscape or deliberately provoke surprise or tension with the surroundings.
6. Do not worry if there is no immediate response. The process of exploring is as important as the product. It is common for young people who do not consider themselves artistic to be inspired by this activity. Occasionally it helps for two or three persons to work together on a piece of land art.
7. On completion, encourage them to visit each other's work as

part of the natural gallery. Allow each person the opportunity to talk about their work, their inspiration, ideas and how they made it. Some may wish to record their work by sketching or photographing.

8. Have a final group review about their response to the activity and whether it achieved its aims. Discuss whether to leave the work *in situ* or to return things as far as possible to their original setting.

Although Andy Goldsworthy is perhaps Britain's best known 'land artist', there are others who work with a similar sensitive approach to the environment and whose art demonstrates a strong personal connection.

Richard Long is an artist who records his journeys across the landscape in lines or circles made from local materials such as rocks or mud. He maps his walks using words to express events on his journey or his response to the land. He sometimes juxtaposes the description of his walk with the more conventional list of places he has visited on the journey (see Fuchs 1986). This technique can be used to help young people understand that we relate to and value places in the landscape through our own personal experiences.

The following case study describes how a critical study of one artist's work can be used as a basis for young people to explore the environment, gain first-hand experience and through practical activities make their own personal response.

Case study—Prayer for the environment

Bryan Edmondson, an artist and educationist based in the Wigan area, uses the work of the Scottish artist, Eileen Lawrence, as a stimulus for one of his workshops with young people. Eileen produces long, narrow prayer sticks, reminiscent of those found in Tibet, exquisitely painted with details of natural objects found on her walks in Scotland. On paper produced from natural materials she paints intricate images of feathers, grasses, birds' eggs etc which represent personal events in her exploration of wild places. The details are stunning and we can recognise shapes and forms which are repeated throughout the natural world.

Bryan uses Eileen's work as a model to encourage participants to create their own work within a similar format. Young people investigate and record experiences in a small environment by making drawings, writing , taking texture rubbings and collecting materials, leaves, petals, seeds etc. to use in collage. By arranging these elements on a range of backing papers, many of them recycled from paper bags, they create their individual prayers for the environment. These can be left as single pieces but can also be joined together, end to end to make a long prayer roll, a dramatic statement of a group's response to the environment.

Bryan has used this workshop successfully with different groups. He believes that Eileen Lawrence's work provides a structure which acts as a safety net for less confident young people. Those not sure of their drawing skills have a range of alternatives through collage. The workshop provides an opportunity for everyone to make a visual statement expressing their personal feelings about the environment.

From my experience, young people relate very readily and enthusiastically to the use of the visual arts in encouraging environmental awareness. Art is no longer confined to galleries and frequently occurs in outdoor environments, for example, sculptures are found in country parks, forests and in towns. There are many opportunities for outdoor leaders, whether based in towns or in the countryside, to make contact with local artists who are interested in the environment. Artists may interpret the environment in different ways and their work can provoke interest and understanding and occasionally may inspire young people.

Creative writing

The outdoors is a wonderful source of inspiration for writing. Young people are away from their usual surroundings and are introduced to new activities, environments and situations. Outdoor experiences can be powerful and may involve physical and mental effort and lead to emotional responses. Writing is a way of expressing and recording feelings and situations. It can also help in reviewing the experience.

Some young people may not enjoy reading and writing and may associate it with schoolwork. There are a number of ways in which leaders can encourage the joy of writing and use the environment to stimulate their interest. Leaders do not have to be English specialists or wordsmiths. If you are open-minded and enthusiastic it is well within your ability to introduce these ideas to young people. Here are some guidelines:

1. Introduce good environmental writing to young people when occasions arise in the outdoors
A few examples are given here to illustrate this: After heavy rain in mountainous areas Robert Southey's poem, *The Cataract of Lodore*, is a way of capturing the sounds and the movement of water. Southey wrote the poem in response to the question: 'How does the water come down at Lodore?'

> . . . Showering and springing,
> Flying and flinging,

> Writhing and ringing,
> Eddying and whisking,
> Spouting and frisking,
> Turning and twisting,
> Around and around
> With endless rebound!
>
> Dizzying and deafening the ear with its sound

Gerard Manley Hopkins' poem, *Inversnaid*, is another one to be read aloud. It rings with the sound of tumbling water:

> This darksome burn, horseback brown,
> His rollrock highroad roaring down,
> In coop and in comb the fleece of his foam
> Flutes and low to the lake falls home.

Some writing can draw attention to elements in a landscape. Norman Nicholson, lived in Millom in Cumbria and has written much about the urban and rural landscape. He makes fine and detailed observations of the rocks, weather, old industries, farms, forest, lakes and mountains. He describes the cottages of the Lake District:

Lakeland cottages were not built for the sake of the view; nor were they built to be looked at. They were essentially homes, built to give shelter in what then was—and on a November night still is—a bleak and inhospitable climate. They are therefore as inconspicuous as possible. The farms of the upper fells squat and cower in the dips of little gills or corries or huddle like a sheep close to an overhanging rock.

There are examples of good regional writing from all over Britain and it is worth collecting a few poems or short passages of prose to read in the outdoors when the situation is right.

Some writers have managed to capture special moments in the outdoors and paint wonderful images with their words. Here is an example from Berlie Doherty, a writer based in the Peak District. It describes a magical experience whilst exploring a cave in the dark with a group of young people. A solitary candle is lit:

The Cave-moth

> I remember Damian
> The bearer of candle-light
> In the cave's dark.
> He was a white moth
> His face flickered
> Bewildered and proud
> He floated
> Towards the hush of our whispers
> He was a dislocated glow

Lifting away
Night's thickness into thin air
Spreading away
The roof and walls
The weight of mountains
With his brief flame.

2. Encourage young people to jot down their thoughts or ideas or keep a diary or log of their outdoor experiences

They may record a new experience such as entering a cave for the first time or canoeing their first rapid. What senses did they use?

What did you hear?
Example: 'the rush of water as the rapid approached, the echo ringing around the cave, the hollow drips of water.'

What did you smell?
Example: 'the frothy, earthiness of the river or dank staleness of the cave.'

What did you feel?
Example: 'the spray in my face, the water sucking and bouncing my boat, the cold blast of air on leaving the cave.'

What did you see?
Example: 'the endless motion of the rapids, the eddies spiralling at the sides, the disappearing speck of light as we descended the shaft.'

Ask them to describe their own emotions—there may be uncertainty, expectation, fear, a release of energy, a sense of achievement?

These are good starting points to elicit personal responses through writing notes, phrases or even words that will trigger memories.

3. Give them a pattern or structure to help in their writing

Terry Gifford is a poet and a Senior Lecturer at Bretton Hall College, Leeds University; he is also a climber and environmentalist. Each year he runs writers' workshops for young people using the outdoors for inspiration. He encourages them to use new forms of writing, such as the amulet, to give them confidence and help their writing. Terry reads out his ecological amulet, *Bat Charm*, on the fells to show young people how everything in nature is connected to everything else:

Bat Charm

Inside the bat the highest sound
Inside the highest sound an echo
Inside the echo a mountain of meanings
Inside the mountain a wet cave
Inside the wet cave a dry chamber
Inside the dry chamber a grooved roof
Inside the grooved roof a leather pouch
Inside the leather pouch a bat
Inside the bat the highest sound.
                    Terry Gifford (1991)

Using the amulet to give structure James Hill, a 15 year old, responded with this fine piece of writing reminiscent of William Blake's To See a World in a Grain of Sand:

> Reduce a breathing mountain, find a spawning boulder.
> Reduce a spawning boulder, find a minion rock.
> Reduce a minion rock, find a pebbly stone.
> Reduce a pebbly stone, find a rough gravel.
> Reduce a rough gravel, find a grain of sand.
> Reduce a grain of sand, find a breathing mountain.
> Reduce a breathing mountain, find a spawning boulder.

Another type of poetry which gives a simple structure is haiku, a traditional Japanese form. It tries to capture an image or a thought in just three lines with a total of 17 syllables. The usual structure is:

Line One: Sets the scene (five syllables).
Line Two: Develops the theme (seven syllables).
Line Three: A thought or reflection on the first two lines (five syllables).

Here are a few examples:

> First snow of winter
> Covering the old town tip
> Children shriek with joy.

> The full blast of wind
> Whips up a curtain of spray
> We shrink below deck.

> A delicate frond
> Gradually unfolding
> To announce the spring.

Shape poems or word pictures are great fun and can sometimes give an incentive to those reluctant to put pen to paper (figure 6.1).

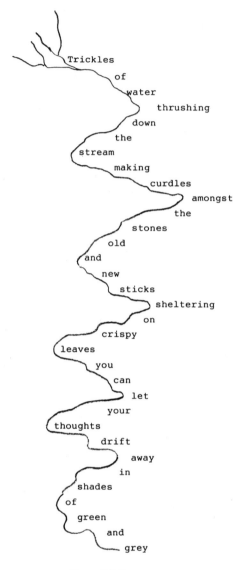

*Figure 6.1.*Shape poem

7. Working together—From groups to communities

Introduction

A personal connection with the environment may be the stimulus for interest and concern but effective action will depend on people working together in groups and communities. The importance of social skills such as trust, communication, co-operation and negotiation in helping to empower young people was discussed in an earlier section. These skills are essential in educating for sustainability (see ten essential competencies page 17).

Working together.

It has long been recognised that outdoor leaders can play a key role in social development, by encouraging groups to work together, share ideas and help each other. This can be the basis for developing higher level social skills where young people take responsibility for organising their own groups. An extension of this is where they participate as a member of a community using each other's strengths in working towards a common goal.

The role of outdoor leaders

Outdoor leaders have clear advantages in developing young people's social skills. They operate outside the formal structures of school, college or work, often in new and interesting environments. They usually have small groups which allows for good social interaction. Time is not a problem and experiences may be intense. In many cases emphasis will not be on gaining knowledge but on expressing feelings and clarifying attitudes and values. Learning can be holistic, involving the mind, body and spirit. There are many opportunities to review and learn from social interaction.

There is little doubt that the very process of placing young people in small groups and providing some exciting activities in a new environment will by itself lead to positive social benefits. But these will be unstructured and haphazard. Outdoor leaders can adopt clear strategies to enhance the development of social skills. Here are a few suggestions.

1. Encourage residential experiences.
2. Involve young people in exercising choice, making decisions and taking responsibility.
3. Emphasise co-operative learning.
4. Choose an appropriate size of group.
5. Choose a focus for the learning.
6. Select appropriate environments.
7. Use an experiential learning model based on planning, doing and reviewing.

Some of these ideas have been discussed in earlier sections, so I will comment on just a few of these below.

The advantages of residential experiences

These experiences involve young people staying away from home for at least one night. They may involve a camp, simple shelters, bivvies or staying at centres. Examples include journeys along the canals using narrow boats or canoes, expeditions across mountains or moorland or the use of fixed bases for fieldwork or outdoor activities. Such residentials are characterised by intense periods of living, working and travelling together. Young people share many tasks which may include planning the residential, buying food, cooking, cleaning, organising their time and route finding. Residentials clearly offer young people a valuable social experience of being part of a small interdependent community for a short period.

Residentials immerse young people into real situations where they need to be flexible and consider other people's needs. They deal with the essentials of life—food, clothing, shelter etc.—and learn to play a role in the group and take responsibility. They see and learn from other members of the group in many informal situations. They may see their leaders in a new light. They meet challenges which may provoke a range of emotions such as joy, disappointment, stress, enthusiasm, anger and empathy. Leaders can help members of the group express and explore these feelings and learn from each situation.

Residentials remove the trappings and comforts of normal life. The individual is prised away from television and computer games and becomes part of an active social group. Meals are not taken in isolation, as is the common practice in many homes, but are shared around a table or campfire. There is the chance to slow down, enjoy conversation and make your own entertainment.

As a result residentials represent critical periods of intense learning for many young people. They offer opportunities for active participation and there is time to develop relationships and reflect on and review experiences. It is difficult to overestimate their importance for social development.

Leaders can also use the residential experience as a basis for understanding the concept of sustainable communities. Two key areas for questions related to residentials are:

1. How successful has the group been in establishing a good community? Have individuals been valued and supported? Has there been open communication? Have resources and responsibilities been shared? Has there been a common goal?
2. Has the experience been sustainable? What energy and raw materials have been consumed? What are the implications locally and globally? Could savings have been made? What has been the impact of the residential on the local environment?

These are the same sort of questions we need to ask if we are interested in creating sustainable communities. Residentials which involve young people in considering the essential necessities of life provide ideal opportunities to raise these issues.

Setting up the experiences

The way leaders set up and facilitate outdoor experiences can influence the development of social skills in their groups. They will probably make decisions regarding the composition of the group, their role as leader and the methods they will use, the focus and aims, the activities offered and the environments used. Let us consider two situations.

Our first leader is action-oriented, he runs a boys' rugby team and chooses his group from the most able and energetic members. He has lots of experience of leading outdoor activities and he is keen to demonstrate his knowledge and expertise. What better way than to jump in a minibus and drive 90 miles up the motorway to his favourite location? Here with the aid of his bag of ropes, karibiners and harnesses he sets up an abseil for the group and allows them to enjoy a new experience under his control. Later in the same day the group hire mountain bikes and take on the challenge of how high they can get up an old Roman road across an area of moorland. The lads appear to thrive on the competition. They return late and speed home to the city. It has been a fun day, they are exhausted.

The second leader has a group of mixed sex and ability from the city. She wants to encourage as much group work as possible. She designs a problem-solving activity which involves the group in planning and sharing responsibility. They have to visit various parts of the city, for example the highest point, the site of the oldest rocks, an ancient monument and a modern sculpture to solve the problem. They can travel on foot or by public transport but they are limited in their spending. The group's success depends on smaller groups of two and three collecting clues and coming back together to jointly solve the problem. The leader is available at pre-arranged places during the day for consultation. At the end the group meet for a barbecue by the canal to review the experience. The leader recognises that this part of the day is as important as the activity itself.

Activity—Two leaders

Discuss the two case studies outlined above in terms of:

- roles of the leaders
- responsibilities of group members
- focus of the experiences
- impact on the environment
- level of enjoyment
- the development of social skills

Developing the group

Groups of young people coming together for the first time will develop naturally. However, the group's time may be limited and it is the leader's role to set the scene and act as a catalyst or facilitator for the group. There are a number of well-known techniques to encourage the process of group development. Leaders often start with ice-breakers, simple activities designed to exchange greetings, learn names and give confidence to individuals. 'Common Tree' is a good example of an ice-breaker. It is interactive, visual, non-threatening and linked to an environmental theme:

As the group is established it is important for the leader to encourage trust and opportunities for individuals to develop self-esteem and confidence. Here are two simple activities, 'Blowing in the Wind' and 'Blindfold Caterpillar', which help to do this:

Activity—Common tree

Attach a large sheet of paper to a wall. It should be large enough for five or six people to use it at the same time. An outline of a tree is sketched on the paper.

Ask participants to introduce themselves to each other in pairs and to find as many attributes, interests etc. as possible that they have in common, for example, 'we both like modern art', 'we enjoy camping'. Each pair chooses one commonality to put on the tree in the form of a large leaf and adds their names to it. They then introduce themselves to new people and add another leaf until every member of the group has met and talked to each other. The group's 'Common Tree' should then be covered with leaves.

The tree can be left on the wall and added to later. It makes for a lively introduction and represents a group activity that combines co-operation and creativity. It may be the group's first achievement.

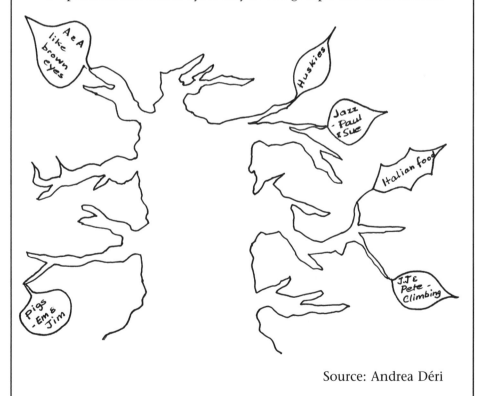

Source: Andrea Déri

Activity—Blowing in the wind

A group of about six people make a tight circle, shoulder to shoulder. One person stands in the middle, with feet together and eyes closed. They represent a tree that is gently swayed, silently by the wind, around and across the circle, supported by the hands of the other member's of the group. The tree can sway and bend in the wind but must not be allowed to fall, it should be supported gently and kept in continuous motion. The person relaxes as the tree moves silently and flexibly from side to side. After a few minutes the tree is changed until each person has had a turn in the centre of the circle. This is an excellent trust activity and all the group work closely together.

Activity—Blindfold caterpillar

A group of about 12 people form a caterpillar by joining in a line, holding on to each other's waists. Each becomes a segment of the caterpillar and all are blindfolded except the person in front, the head of the caterpillar. The leader indicates a route for the caterpillar to follow which might take the animal under branches, over logs and through bushes. The head of the caterpillar directs the group by verbal instructions. Change the heads several times until the group moves proficiently.

The activity can be extended and made more complex by asking the group to review their success and the problems they encountered. Then suggest they devise a non-verbal language that can be used by the new head of the caterpillar to move it along a chosen route. The head cannot touch any of the group or use their voice. Allow the group to make changes to their non-verbal messages and change the head of the caterpillar.

This is a good activity to review. Ask the group what personal and social qualities where brought out by the activity. They should identify the three key qualities of trust, co-operation and communication.

As an alternative before introducing 'blindfold caterpillar' ask the group, divided into smaller groups of four or five persons, to brainstorm all the personal and social qualities they can, producing a list quickly. Every idea is put down at this stage, nothing is discarded. From this, each small group identifies the three qualities they consider to be the most important. They then join the other groups who have identified their three skills and the whole group negotiate to determine their final three qualities.

Then try the 'blindfold caterpillar' as described above and review the personal and social qualities encouraged by the activity. Compare these with the three qualities discussed and negotiated by the groups.

The above activities allow the group to develop and interact physically and mentally in informal situations outdoors. Trust, co-operation and improved self-esteem will lead to better communication. An individual who feels confident and who has the mutual support of a strong group can express ideas openly. Effective communication is the most important skill in educating for sustainability. 'Identileaf' is an environmental awareness activity which encourages teamwork and communication:

Activity—Identileaf

In groups of five or six participants, choose 12 leaves from the local environment. If possible collect leaves that have fallen on the ground. They should represent a full range of size and shape. Each group chooses their own name for each leaf, avoiding any reference to the actual or scientific name. The name chosen should relate to the appearance, shape, touch or smell of the leaf. It should not be too obscure but challenge the other groups to use their senses and powers of deduction. Write the 12 names on a sheet of paper and give this with the leaves to another group. They must identify the leaves using your list of names. When all groups have had a turn to identify each other's leaves they can be fixed onto large sheets of paper and displayed.

An alternative to this is to ask groups to devise a simple system of classification, like an identification key for the 12 leaves. They could be divided and subdivided according to size, colour, shape, smoothness etc. and each leaf still given a name. No pictures should be drawn. Give the identification system with the leaves to the other groups.

In this activity groups need to think clearly and negotiate over their choice of names and systems of identification. The aim is to communicate meaning not to confuse the other groups.

Source: Sue Townsend

Trust, co-operation and good communication are essential social skills which help groups to develop smoothly. This applies to temporary groups as well as communities. If leaders are interested in sustainability it is also important to encourage groups to think about and plan for the future. 'Group Visions' is an example of an activity designed to promote futures thinking.

Activity—Group visions

In small groups of three or four persons, young people record along a time line on a large sheet of paper the personal and other events that have had a significant impact on their lives from their birth to the present time. The personal influences can be written above the line and the other events—local, national or global—can be written below the line. The groups will need to be selective and agree on their choices.

The time line is continued into the future along three separate lines (see below). One line shows the group's vision for the future in terms of their personal lives. The second line shows their vision for their community. The third line shows their preferred view of the world.

This activity helps young people to put their own lives into context and to appreciate the connections between personal, community and global considerations. It also encourages them to think about alternatives and to feel that they can make changes which may shape their own and other people's futures.

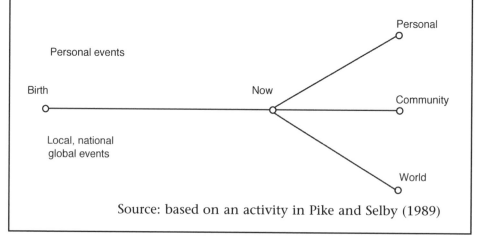

Source: based on an activity in Pike and Selby (1989)

Another way to encourage young people to think about the future is by drawing up action plans. Small groups can discuss how they can take action to improve their group, their community, their region or country, the world. They should attach a timescale to their actions: 'What can they do now; in three months' time; in six months' time?' (see opposite).

Involving young people in their local environment

A belief that runs through this book is that the environment begins on our doorsteps and environmental education is about people and their actions rather than about plants, animals and spectacular landscapes. It is about how

Planning action

Action	Now	In three months	In six months
Group			
Community			
Region/country			
World			

we become aware, interested, concerned and involved with environments and communities. There is a strong temptation to ignore our local environment, which for many young people is the built up areas of the city or suburbs, and to take off to more beautiful, distant environments. I have argued that these remoter, more natural areas can and do inspire young people and help them feel connected to the earth. Leaders should not deny their groups such experiences. But local environments provide obvious starting points for group involvement and action. It is essential that leaders relate their groups' experiences to their home environment, wherever they take place.

Many people have little knowledge of the history, architecture or traditions of their own neighbourhoods. They may feel they have little influence over changes that occur. They are removed from the decisions made by 'planners', 'councillors' or 'government'. Our task as leaders is to empower groups, to help them to work well together and to encourage them to become involved in their own communities and environments. The following activities should provide leaders with ideas to introduce this process:

Activity—Community map

1. In groups of about four or five persons walk around your local neighbourhood talking about the places which are important to you. Decide where you would make the boundaries of the community.
2. In the same groups, draw a large map of your community. This can be done by joining large sheets of paper together on the floor and drawing with felt-tipped pens. Do not copy from an existing map, accuracy and scale are not important. The idea is to produce the groups' perception of their community.
3. Put on the map:
   - places you like and dislike
   - landmarks—shops, pubs, your homes, youth centre etc.

- safe and dangerous places
- the boundaries of your community.

4. Ask each person to make a list of ten things they like and ten things they dislike about their community. Discuss these with the other members of the group and agree a group list of ten likes and dislikes.

5. Decide how it might be possible to get rid of your dislikes and to keep or enhance the things your group likes. Here are some examples:

Likes	*Action*
The corner shop.	Support it by shopping there.
The canal bank.	Help with clean-ups.
The old lampposts.	Write and tell your councillor or the planning department.

Dislikes	*Action*
There are no trees.	Contact your local British Trust for Conservation Volunteers or Groundwork Trust for advice with planting.
Difficulties in crossing the road.	Write to the planning department.
Stray dogs.	Contact the RSPCA.

This activity helps to raise awareness of our immediate environment and to discuss our common feelings about the quality of the environment. It begins to consider ways in which the group can take action to improve the environment. An activity which involves the group in a more detailed knowledge and appreciation of their environment is now suggested.

Activity—Community trail

1. In small groups of four or five persons design a trail around your community to show places of interest; distant or surprise views; places which are noisy and those which are quiet; places with strong smells; small features of buildings—windows, doorways, plaques, chimneys; street furniture—letter boxes, fire hydrants, bus stops; unusual or humorous signs; places which are cared for and places which are neglected; old and new buildings; local stones and manufactured materials; unusual shapes—arches, spires, domes etc. You should choose places which reflect positive and negative aspects of the townscape.

2. Your community trail is like a nature trail. Draw a map and give instructions to get from one point to the next. Include about ten stopping places where you will ask the participants to observe, record or comment on something. You may choose a theme for your trail.

3. Designing the trail and writing the instructions will involve the group in detailed observation and discussion in their local environment. This will be an important part of learning about their environment and give them insights into their community. It may identify features that are worth protecting or sites which could be improved.

Encouraging a sense of community

Young people can extend these ideas to involve the whole community in finding out more about their immediate environment. They could invite local people to try their trail and ask for comments. Another approach is to draw up a questionnaire and interview different individuals to find out what they like, dislike and would like to improve in their environment. It is likely that different interests will be expressed by different age groups. For example, children's concerns may be related to play and entertainment, whereas older people may be concerned about better public transport and safety in the community. The results of such a survey, together with photographs, drawings and comments could form the basis of a local exhibition put up at the community centre or library. If there is sufficient interest this could lead to the setting up of a community action group to work for environmental improvements.

At this stage it may be possible to enlist the help of professionals to act as a catalyst and give impetus to the project. There are organisations which may offer ideas and support. 'Common Ground' has, for many years tried to encourage stronger links between communities and their local environments. They help people to become aware of distinctive features of their local areas which make one place different from another. These do not need to be rare or spectacular things and they can be large or small for example, a window, a fruit tree, a viewpoint, a pond, a chimney, a patch of wild flowers. 'Common Ground' have developed projects using the arts to encourage people to explore, record and celebrate some of these local features that they appreciate. By recognising that often commonplace things are valued, it helps to conserve these everyday environments and to strengthen community feelings.

One project, pioneered by 'Common Ground', is the idea of creating a 'Parish map' to celebrate local distinctiveness. Communities meet to share their thoughts and feelings about their environment and to make a map of the things that are special to them. This does not need to be a map in the traditional sense but can be a collage, an embroidery, a painting, a series of photographs or even a performance. Sometimes artists encourage or inspire these projects but they are essentially about local people getting involved. Parish maps help to link people with places, they show the richness and variety of places, how places are shaped by nature and culture and they encourage people to take responsibility for their local area. Since the project was established in 1987 hundreds of parish maps have been made throughout Britain and people have fought to protect special features of their landscapes and taken action themselves to improve their environment.

8. Treading lightly—Sustainable use of the outdoors

We abuse land because we regard it as a commodity belonging to us. When we see land as a community to which we belong we may then be able to use it with love and respect.

Aldo Leopold (1949)

Gymnasium, laboratory or sacred space?

There are many reasons why leaders bring young people into the outdoors. For some it is a recreational experience or a chance to develop physical skills in such activities as canoeing or rock climbing. Others come to study aspects of an environment relating their work to the school or college curriculum. Whilst for others the outdoors provides the basis for developing personal and social development.

There is a danger that each group may simply use the environment as a backcloth for its own aims. Sometimes the use is selfish, resulting in environmental damage or interference with other people's enjoyment. Some groups still treat the countryside as a gymnasium for demonstrating their physical prowess. Summits exist to be 'conquered' and gulleys 'bashed'. They travel in haste, shout their instructions and are oblivious to the natural world around them. Field study groups are not necessarily more sensitive and they may treat the environment as a laboratory for their experiments and investigations. There are examples of damage to geological sites, disturbance to wildlife and pestering of local residents with questionnaire surveys.

How can we create a more sensitive approach to the environment and encourage groups to interact with it? Robert Hogan (1992) writing about wilderness programmes criticises many for using the environment as no more than a playing field. He argues that wilderness areas are very special places that can tap a spiritual dimension and transform people. He relates these environments to the psychiatrist Carl Jung's concept of 'Sacred Space', a place pervaded by a sense of power and mystery that can lead to positive empowerment. This is

Treading lightly.

closely related to Jean Liedloff's 'glade' mentioned earlier (page 64). The environments we use with our groups may not offer the potential of wilderness but they should still be presented as special places. Our groups are the guests, not there to abuse or compete, but to be made welcome and to feel at home. If we take this approach and at the same time encourage an awareness and understanding of the special places we are travelling through, there is little doubt that our groups will benefit from feeling connected.

The impact of outdoor activities

The Dartington Amenity Research Trust report, *Groups in the Countryside*, published in 1980 recognised the rapid growth in demand for a wide range of group activities in the countryside. The report estimated that in England and Wales there were 20 million person-days devoted to field studies, outdoor pursuits and other group activities. These activities were concentrated in particular areas, about 40% took place in National Parks and there was evidence of many popular sites being over used. The report stated that groups of young people in the countryside were a potential threat to wildlife, communities and the landscape. There is little doubt that since 1980 the number of groups using the countryside has continued to grow and in some areas pressures have increased considerably.

What forms does this impact take? It is possible to distinguish a number of different kinds of pressure:

Physical impact
At one extreme this could result from wilful damage to property or thoughtless actions such as climbing walls, dumping litter or lighting fires. More commonly it is a result of the general wear and tear associated with group activities which may lead, for example, to footpath erosion and damage to surfaces by horse riding and mountain biking.

Ecological impact
This includes disturbance or damage to wildlife. Again this might be wilful, for example in collecting eggs or rare species of plants but it is more often a result of ignorance. Sometimes there is unnecessary trampling of sites with rare species of insects or plants or disturbance to nesting birds on crag, moorland or water.

Social impact
This may represent the most significant impact of outdoor groups. The Hunt Report (1989), *In Search of Adventure*, identified the following pressures sometimes faced by local communities:

1. Noise, particularly at night, which may be exacerbated by drunkenness and foul language.
2. Litter and occasionally thoughtless or deliberate vandalism.

3. Fieldwork and surveys which involve questioning local people.
4. Intimidating or aggressive behaviour and theft of property.
5. Dangerous driving, either by students if they have use of personal transport, or by staff.
6. Lack of understanding of, and respect for, the local culture or way of life such as failure to respect the Sabbath.
7. Damage to the livelihood of farmers by leaving gates open, damaging walls and fences, disturbing stock.
8. Wide games which are often carried out at night to test problem-solving skills or map-reading.
9. Overcrowding of shops, inns and other local facilities.

This is a catalogue of disturbance, but the Hunt Report does point out that such difficulties are not widely experienced. They occur most often when outdoor activities are based close to small communities and are poorly managed.

Psychological impact
This is a more difficult concept and harder to measure. It occurs when one group's activities affect the experience and enjoyment of other people in the outdoors. For example, a large noisy group paddling along a canal could impose themselves on people who had come to enjoy the tranquillity from fishing or bird watching. Some places, such as a cave or a deep narrow valley may quickly become crowded when several groups arrive together and this detracts from the experience. Walkers sometimes claim that the presence of mountain bikers on the fells affects their enjoyment. Large-scale events, such as orienteering, fell running or mountain marathons may be inappropriate in some environments enjoyed for their peace and quiet.

Footpath erosion is not vandalism

We need to put the impact of groups in the outdoors into context. It is often difficult to separate the group impact from that of the general public or local residents. There is also the danger that we may concentrate our concern on the most obvious visual or physical problems whereas the ecological, social or psychological impact may be more significant. We get upset about litter: rightly so, it is an eyesore and represents an uncaring attitude to our environment. However, it does not represent permanent damage and it can usually be cleared without too much difficulty.

Footpath erosion has also become a major issue in some areas. There are certainly unattractive scars worn by thousands of eager feet on our more popular hills and mountains. But footpath erosion is not vandalism. It represents people getting away from their vehicles and discovering the countryside for themselves. It is a management problem. In many cases paths can be repaired, vegetation recovers and people can be encouraged to use other routes or to visit less popular areas. I am not claiming that solutions

are always easy. For example, along some very popular long-distance footpaths, such as the Pennine Way, artificial surfaces have been laid to cope with the pressure and some of this work is extremely time consuming and expensive. But this type of damage is not irreparable.

Ecological damage is not always so obvious. It is often difficult to assess disturbance from outdoor activities on particular environments. A joint Countryside Commission and Sports Council study, *Sport, Recreation and Nature Conservation*, published in 1988 concluded that for a variety of outdoor activities disturbance and damage was relatively insignificant although local impacts can be serious. In contrast, studies of sensitive environments, such as moorlands of national ecological importance, suggest that group impact can be detrimental. In 1990 the Peak District National Park published a report by Penny Anderson, *Moorland Recreation and Wildlife in the Peak District*, which found that several summer breeding birds, such as curlew, golden plover and common sandpiper, are easily disturbed by recreational use particularly away from paths. The report also suggested that moorland plants, especially woody species and those growing on wet peat were susceptible to trampling. It argued that recreational use of some areas was exceeding the natural carrying capacities. The case study on the use of gills for rock scrambling illustrates how particular environments can be very sensitive to use but also how environmental awareness can alleviate the problems.

It is important to put environmental and social problems caused by outdoor groups in the more general context of wider pressures on the environment. John Gittins (1990) makes this point clearly:

... when put against the more general and fundamental environmental changes taking place—globally, for example, climatic change, acid rain and the destruction of rain forests; and in the British countryside, in particular, such as the removal of hedgerows, loss of wetlands, the afforestation of moorland, the excessive use of pesticides and herbicides, the loss of Green Belt areas, rural depopulation and the loss of services in rural areas—the impact of young people participating in adventure activities is negligible. Even the Council for the Preservation of Rural England, a strong conservationist body, states: 'the balance of advantage lies firmly in extending and enhancing the opportunities for young people to enjoy the countryside ... through such experiences they will come to appreciate and care for the survival of our countryside.'

It can be argued that those young eager feet eroding the paths belong to young people who will fight to protect the environment in the future.

Case study—Outdoor activities in a sensitive environment. The Lake District gills

The Lake District gills are a very special environment. They are the steep rocky valleys that descend from the mountains associated mainly with lines of weakness in the Borrowdale Volcanic series of rocks. In total they occupy just ten hectares of land, a tiny portion of the uplands. Unlike other areas they have not suffered the effects of sheep grazing and represent a remnant of the former upland vegetation. The ecologist, Bob Bunce who has studied the gills for many years, points out that they have a very rich flora but their uniqueness is the variety of plants from different habitats found in close proximity. As you ascend the gills you find a succession of woodland, meadow and arctic–alpine species. Nowhere else in Britain does such a mixture occur.

The nature of the gills, with their sheer sides, waterfalls and rock-strewn beds makes them dramatic environments to travel through. Gill scrambling is an exciting activity and one that has become popular over the last 15 years, especially with the publication of guidebooks and use by outdoor centre groups. Concern over this growing use led to the establishment of a 'gill group' who put forward a set of guidelines for outdoor leaders. These are now incorporated into a leaflet published by the Lake District National Park. There are five simple rules.

1. Keep to the rocky bed of the gill.
2. Groups should keep in line.
3. Leave plants for others to enjoy.
4. Avoid crumbling rock.
5. Follow only established routes.

> This raised awareness amongst outdoor leaders and many have
> been keen to convey the uniqueness of these environments to their
> groups. The adventure experience is enriched by this understand-
> ing. A recent study by Fay Beasley (1997) concludes that 'the efforts
> of groups of interested parties over the past 15 years to raise
> awareness of users to the ecological and conservational importance
> of Lakeland gills has generally been successful.' This case study
> demonstrates how conservationists and outdoor enthusiasts can
> work together through mutual understanding and good communi-
> cation.

Lessening the impact

The use of the gills by organised groups is largely a success story. It
demonstrates how the raising of awareness amongst leaders about the
significance and fragility of these environments can lead to changes of
attitudes and practice. The Gill Group and Lake District National Park have
not been heavy handed in their approach, there are no 'Keep Out' signs.
Instead a leaflet explains the value of the gills and offers a simple set of
guidelines. These have been accepted by leaders.

As part of the Hunt Report (1989) a questionnaire survey was sent to users
and providers of outdoor activities. One question asked: What steps do you
take to avoid inconvenience to the local community or damage to the
environment? There were 342 respondents and their comments can be
summarised in terms of:

- adequate staff training and careful supervision of young people;
- education of young people, raising environmental awareness and following
  codes of conduct;
- close liaison with environmental groups and good public relations with the
  local community, especially landowners;
- by choice of sites and control over the use of sensitive areas.

These comments indicate that there is a growing environmental awareness
and concern amongst outdoor leaders. This is reflected in an increasing
commitment to conservation from the professional bodies involved in
outdoor education and the national governing bodies of the various outdoor
sports. All these organisations appreciate the need for the sustainable use of
the outdoors. One organisation which has been active in this field for nearly
15 years is the Adventure and Environmental Awareness Group.

The Adventure and Environmental Awareness Group

How many adventurers are aware of the delicate ecological balance and
beauty of the environment through which they journey? Does the climber

know or care about the mountain plants clinging to the steep rock faces? Do canoeists relate to the world of water birds and otters as they travel down rivers? Do the field-study groups, sampling vegetation and measuring their river channels, develop any feelings for the natural world? How many of us accept responsibility for the environment and are prepared to take steps towards its conservation?

The Group, established in 1984, is comprised of a wide range of representatives from outdoor education and national and regional recreation and conservation interests. The Group's aim is: 'to encourage awareness, understanding and concern for the natural environment amongst those involved with adventure, education and recreation.'

The Group believes that direct experience in the outdoors encourages an interest in conservation and at the same time greater awareness of the richness and interrelatedness of the environment enhances the outdoor experience. It tries to achieve these aims through workshops, talks, publicity and conferences and by forging links between outdoor enthusiasts and environmentalists.

Early workshops were aimed at communicating the need for a more sensitive approach to the environment to as wide an audience as possible. It is clear that an awareness of the impact of one's own activities often leads to greater care and respect. Over the years the Group has acted as a catalyst in bringing diverse interests together to raise awareness and encourage more sustainable use of the outdoors. It has organised a series of conferences to consider the impact of particular user groups, such as climbers, canoeists and mountain bikers on the environment. These have led to guidelines and codes of good practice. As an example, the Group's report on *Mountain Biking and the Environment* gives a clear statement of the issues from the viewpoints of practitioners and conservationists and sets out recommendations for improved route networks in less sensitive environments. This report stimulated a national debate on this issue and led to the setting up of a Mountain Biking Liaison Group in the Lake District National Park. More recently a joint conference with the Friends of the Lake District entitled 'Large-scale Events in the Countryside' has succeeded in drawing attention to the growing number of large orienteering, fell-running, mountain biking and multi-activity events which can have considerable impact in quiet areas of the countryside. The aim of such conferences is not to hammer the user groups with a catalogue of complaints but to encourage awareness of the balance of nature and the benefits of adopting more sensitive and sustainable approaches.

The Group's most recent workshop was aimed at encouraging outdoor leaders to place more emphasis on environmental education. The workshop produced many good ideas:

There is a tension between adventure and environment. Adventure is about uncertainty and challenge. The environment, in the form of wind, waves, white water, crag, fell or forest may provide the challenge. We pit ourselves against these natural elements, there is the excitement of real or perceived risk, we overcome the challenge and we enjoy the 'buzz' of success. At worst we are in competition with the environment, at best it provides simply the backcloth for our activities. How can the outdoor leader of 11–16 year olds turn the self-centred 'buzz' into a more outgoing awareness of and interest in the environment? How can we get away from the one or two token environmental sessions thrown into an outdoor programme to add a little variety, meet some curriculum needs or help with staffing problems?

These were the questions addressed by the recent workshop. The day did not produce all of the answers but the workshop did suggest how leaders can encourage environmental awareness and how our programmes can be improved. Here are some guidelines:

1. Recognise the link between personal, social and environmental education. If there is low self-esteem and little respect for others, there is unlikely to be much chance of developing environmental awareness and respect. The work of outdoor leaders in personal and social development is fundamental to environmental education which is concerned with changing attitudes and encouraging individual responsibility. Outdoor leaders can play a key role in this process.
2. Introduce good environmental practice into the whole organisation and its programmes rather than through isolated activities. The outdoor leader is a powerful role model. Show enthusiasm for the environment and demonstrate through your own interest and practice.
3. Help the group to appreciate the special qualities of each environment, encourage a 'sense of place' through an understanding of geology, ecology and history. Interpret the landscape but do not lecture. Focus on the detail of the environment—a lichen, a rock, an eddy, a web, a leaf. Use different senses to explore the environment. Encourage a personal response through art, poetry, discussion or drama. In other words, help people to connect with place.
4. Outdoor experiences through climbing, caving, canoeing or sailing bring young people in close contact with the weather and the natural environment and help them develop a sense of awe and wonder. Such feelings can motivate and make young people more receptive to environmental education.
5. Raise issues such as access, land use and conservation and consider the group's impact on the environment but do not concentrate unduly on problems. Be positive, remember this particular group has not caused all the problems. Our aim is enjoyment, awareness and understanding.
6. Adopt a more sensitive approach to activities. Promote the concept of journey and exploration rather than the 'thrash, dash, trash' approach. Thrills may have their place, but avoid a programme based on a series of quick fixes.
7. Reflection and reviewing can help young people put their experiences into the wider context of other people and the world around us. Choose the time and place carefully, a quiet time for reflection and discussion after an active, exciting session can challenge attitudes and actions towards the environment.

Codes of good practice

One successful method of raising awareness of environmental issues and suggesting appropriate action is through guidelines and codes of practice. Drawing up guidelines is not always an easy task but it helps to focus attention on the needs of the environment and how we can use the outdoors sustainably.

An early effort by a national governing body, the British Mountaineering Council, at producing environmental guidelines is their joint publication with the Nature Conservancy Council called, *Tread Lightly* published in 1988. Since then other national bodies for outdoor sports, such as fell running, canoeing and caving, have produced statements and codes on their use of the environment. Recently some organisations have put forward 'charters' asking for stronger commitments from their members. The Pembrokeshire Outdoor Charter, drawn up by activity and education centres operating in the national park, is an example. Members agree to abide by the charter and as a result gain accreditation.

The problem with some of these codes is that they are narrow in concept and written in a negative way, for example, 'do not enter private land without permission', 'we will discuss implications with the National Park before spreading activities into sites or areas which are currently unused', 'when in groups it is better to walk in single file on the path than line abreast'. I believe that codes should be much more positive in their presentation and should try to encourage learning about and for the environment. As an example consider the following 'Ten Steps' as simple guidelines for outdoor leaders to encourage environmental awareness and good practice:

Ten steps

1. Let your group know they are in a special place. Tell them about the local environment.
2. Show your group some of the wonders of life around them. Let them use their senses.
3. Give them an understanding about how plants, animals and ourselves are interdependent.
4. Discuss some of the issues affecting the conservation of landscape and wildlife.
5. Encourage them to tread lightly and to cause as little damage as possible to plants, animals and rocks. Leave a site cleaner than you found it.
6. Work with small groups. Encourage them to travel quietly and to respect the interests of people who live and work in the countryside.

7. Avoid habitats which are particularly sensitive to disturbance.
8. Respect rights of way, local by-laws and access agreements.
9. Consider the method of transport to a site. Respect others and the environment when parking and if you use equipment.
10. Encourage practical conservation to put something back.

Adopting more sensitive approaches

In Britain we have a strong tradition of using the environment for adventure, scientific research and character building. We have seen how these approaches have taken their toll. In Scandanavia, a quite different tradition of 'Friluftsliv' or Outdoor Nature Life has developed over the last hundred years. This is a traditional and informal type of outdoor life more in tune with nature. Long walking and skiing tours throughout the year are a part of Norwegian culture. Atle Tellnes (1993) argues that Friluftsliv can create a base for environmental consciousness, good health, higher quality of life and sustainable development. Gunnar Repp (1996) also stresses the importance of 'good meetings with nature' in developing the whole person, physically, emotionally and intellectually. These experiences not only lead to a rediscovery of nature, in a sensitive way, but may bring about changes in attitudes and a deeper understanding of oneself and other aspects of life.

The philosophy of Friluftsliv is people and nature in harmony, each benefiting the other. Atle Tellnes believes that the deepest experiences result from the following considerations:

- Keeping the group small so that everyone can co-operate and take an active part in decisions as well as responsibility.
- Having people with a variety of backgrounds in the group.
- Choosing areas which are as natural as possible but try to avoid travelling too far to reach them.
- Having sufficient time for the experience.
- Keeping activities close to nature, for example in an open traditional boat, in a tent, around a campfire. Don't build unnecessary technological walls through use of equipment.
- Expedition according to ability but allow for progression. If circumstances are too demanding nature will not be considered as a friend.
- Learning from real situations.
- Allowing time for reflection, reviewing and discussion.

There are clearly some similarities in this list to those suggestions made by the outdoor leaders in the Adventure and Environmental Awareness workshop mentioned earlier. These ideas may be a long way from the outdoor sport enthusiast excited about testing out new machinery and gear and pitting their wits against rock, wind and water. But it should ring true with outdoor leaders interested in developing young people in terms of their hands, hearts and heads.

How do these ideas work out in practice? Let us consider a traditional outdoor activity, mountain walking, and one which many young people do not take to with obvious enthusiasm.

Case study—The mountain

Go climb the mountains and get their good tidings. Nature's peace will flow into you as sunshine flows into trees. The winds will blow their own freshness into you and the storms their energy, while cares will drop off like autumn leaves.

John Muir

Mountains have symbolic significance in many cultures. Climbing mountains is sometimes considered a spiritual journey that takes the traveller closer to the heavens. Many writers have commented on the restorative properties of mountains and that by knowing the mountain you can better know yourself. Mountain climbing and walking are often the focus of outdoor programmes and most outdoor centres are still found in mountainous areas. Mountain activities are often used to encourage skills in leadership and teamwork, they also have great potential in encouraging environmental awareness.

Young people have mixed feelings about mountains. From my experience many teenagers do not take naturally to mountain walking. There is not the immediate excitement associated with other activities, for example canoeing or abseiling. The pleasure, if it exists, requires more patience, more commitment. It may involve a lot of effort in some clumsy, ill-fitting clothes, such as heavy boots and unfashionable anoraks. It can show up differences in levels of fitness and motivation within a group. Although for some the effort and challenge is rewarded with the sense of achievement and enjoyment the journey brings, others will suffer and may not be in a hurry to return. In contrast, most younger children find an experience in the mountains very worthwhile.

There are different approaches to a mountain experience. The macho 'last one to the top is a sissy' approach fortunately no longer receives the favour it did in the past. I can remember my first experience of the mountains:

We could make out the figure of Fat Mac, the history teacher, with a small group of boys some 200 metres below. They'd made the tarn but hadn't the satisfaction of reaching the summit. The rest of us were elated when we joined the others on our descent. They were relieved to be heading down to the coach.

As one of forty schoolboys it was my first experience of the mountains. A three hour bus journey from Liverpool to Great Langdale, a route march along Mickleden and the long slog up Rossett Gill trying to keep pace with the P.E. teacher. The goal was Scafell Pike and we all knew its height. We returned to the city exhausted. I suspect many of the group have never set foot in the mountains again.

Today's groups are better managed and groups of forty are not normally seen in the mountains. But some groups still treat the environment as an assault course and macho leaders exhort their troops to 'conquer' summits. These groups move quickly and noisily and show little interest in the environment around them.

Another approach is the 'teamwork approach', where the group is given the task of route finding through the mountains and the leader follows at some distance. This is a worthwhile exercise and gives the group responsibility for navigation, safety and other aspects of organisation. They make real decisions and there is a sense of achievement in completing the task. However, there is often a sense of urgency to reach their goal and this is not conducive to encouraging environmental awareness.

A third approach is more of a 'journey into the mountains'. It is an exploration, a way of experiencing a mountain environment. It is a gentler approach, respectful of the environment. It is not task-centred in terms of reaching the summit peak or following a given route but puts greater emphasis on a sense of place, getting to know the mountain and its particular environment. There is time to look closely, see the details of a piece of rock, an animal print or bone, time for the group to express their feelings and to absorb the experience. The process of being in the mountains is important, the journey should involve the mind, body and spirit. The following points are suggested as guidelines for creating such a mountain journey:

Choose a route that encourages exploration
The shortest, steepest, most direct route up a mountain is often the least interesting. Choose a route that gently brings your group into the mountains, that allows them to see the mountain from different sides, that does not follow the well-trodden path. Encourage the idea of a journey rather than a 'slog' to the summit.

Vary the terrain, let the group feel the springiness of the heather, the wetness of the bog, find their own hand holes on a rocky ridge. Reduce the overall distance and allow for deviations on the route. Include scrambling sections to add to the adventure.

Reveal the secrets of the mountain
Let the group know they are in a special place, that you think it is special. Show them places that not many others have seen. It could be a favourite tree clinging to a rock face, an outcrop of 'semi-precious' rock, an old sheep fold, an entrance to a mine, a hidden tarn, a spring, a tiny flower, a waterfall, a rock smoothed by the ice, a natural shelter. Every mountain has these special places. These become landmarks on the journey and they inspire questions and interest: 'Why is this here?' 'Who built this?' 'Is this natural or was it made by people?' Good leaders will encourage the young person's natural curiosity.

Fire their imaginations
Sometimes the mountain will inspire the group, at other times the leader may need to provoke the group's interest. One method is to use a few props, for example rock samples to show differences in geology, an old photograph to show how the landscape has changed or a poem to inspire a sense of place. Stories, both true and fiction, can be used to create the atmosphere of former times. Maps can be helpful in interpreting the mountain environment but if over used may get in the way of the real experience.

Make use of water
Plan to include water as part of your journey; if not young people will find it for themselves. Most people like the sound of running water, the taste of a cool mountain stream, the chance to paddle, to build a dam. Understanding rivers is much easier through first-hand experience than from books. After heavy rain water runs down the mountainside in hundreds of small channels that join to form streams which in turn merge to form rivers. Mountains offer good vantage points to see drainage patterns and to appreciate how the landscape has been shaped by the movement of water. There is also the chance to look at the freshwater ecology of a small stream, to consider the different habitats within the stream and discuss simple food chains. Sometimes it is possible to follow a stream up to its source, which may be a spring where the water bubbles to the surface.

Introduce issues
Mountain journeys offer opportunities to discuss environmental issues. Some mountains have suffered damage from over grazing by sheep which has led to changes in vegetation such as the loss of rich heather moorland and its replacement with acid grassland. To understand the reasons for this it is necessary to know something of the political and economic situation and the subsidies available

to hill farmers. Many mountains are in protected landscapes, such as National Parks and there are often issues over the use of the land for recreation, conservation, quarrying, afforestation or water supply. Young people can be introduced to these complex issues and can see the impact of some of these land uses. There is also the chance to consider the need to protect and manage mountain landscapes and to appreciate how decisions are made by governments and landowners and influenced by environmental agencies and pressure groups. I think that all groups should be made aware of the issues regarding their own access to the mountains. Acknowledging this responsibility is an important part of their freedom to enjoy the mountains.

Take time to review

Mountain walking should be conducive to reflection and conversation. Towards the end of a day exploring a mountainous environment the experienced leader can choose a place where the group can get together to review their journey. This might be a viewpoint where the group can focus on the journey they have made, it may be a sheltered hollow away from the wind, the edge of a wood, a sunny glade or an old mine entrance on a wet day. The choice of site is important as it helps to create an atmosphere in which the group can share their thoughts and feelings. There is a chance to reflect on the most and least enjoyable parts of the journey, to reinforce positive aspects of the experience and develop a sense of group achievement.

9. Understanding concepts and issues

Introduction

We have seen that outdoor leaders can play a key role in encouraging young people to enjoy and respond to direct experiences of the environment. They also have much to offer in helping them understand how the natural environment works and how issues arise because of social, economic and political considerations. There is great potential for leaders to support classroom learning and particularly to allow groups to investigate and analyse real issues.

Leaders should not aim to introduce their groups to masses of information as this will lead to confusion and detract from the personal experience. It is important not to duplicate the classroom in the outdoors as the benefits of informality, motivation and enjoyment will be lost. This means that leaders will need to be selective and focus their attention on ideas, concepts and skills of particular value in educating for sustainability. It may be worth referring to the list of competencies presented in chapter 1.

One way leaders can focus their work is to consider the key questions that young people need to answer:

- How does the natural world operate? What are the basic ecological concepts that help us to relate to other life on the earth?
- Who makes the decisions which shape our environments from our backyard to this planet?
- How can we participate in the democratic process?

To tackle these questions leaders need to introduce concepts, encourage enquiry and critical thinking skills and help empower young people to take action for themselves. A good starting point is to consider our ecological links.

Getting connected—Introducing ecology

Many outdoor leaders are apprehensive about teaching aspects of ecology. Their own knowledge may be limited and there is a feeling they need to be able to identify a host of plants and small animals to be a successful teacher. This is far from the case and it is more important that we communicate the main principles of ecology rather than the detailed relationships. Outdoor experiences provide ideal opportunities to teach these principles.

In the early 1970s an American ecologist, Barry Commoner, drew up a set of 'laws of ecology' which help us to understand our relationship with the natural world. These laws provide a useful teaching framework for outdoor leaders. They are:

Introducing ecology.

1. Everything is connected to everything else.
2. Everything has to go somewhere.
3. Everything is always changing.
4. There is no such thing as a free lunch.
5. Everything has limits.

We can consider these concepts in more detail.

Everything is connected

That everything is connected is perhaps the most important concept an outdoor leader can convey. We can think of the earth as a spaceship whose passengers are interdependent. If some passengers are harmed there will be repercussions for the others. Some connections are obvious for example when plants and animals depend on each other for food. The 'food chain', shows such a relationship.

The sun's energy is at the start of all food chains. Producers receive this energy and convert it into food for primary consumers (herbivores). Some of this energy is passed on to secondary consumers (carnivores). When the secondary consumer dies other species help to decompose their bodies and form the final link in the chain. All species are involved in a variety of food chains which are connected to form a 'food web'.

Food is just one of the ways in which plants and animals are connected. We depend on plants for

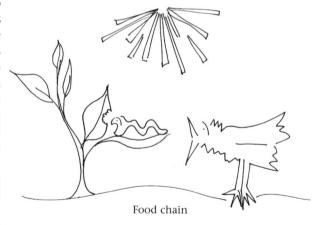

Food chain

the air we breathe and they benefit from the carbon dioxide we exhale. We make use of products from plants and animals for a range of needs and luxuries from clothing, shelter and fuel to medicines. Connections are all around us and it is vital that as leaders we draw attention to this interdependency.

Activity—Getting connected

This is a simple activity to show how different parts of the ecosystem are connected. The leader needs a ball of wool or cord and a set of cards with pictures showing different parts of the ecosystem (sun, soil, water, grass, trees, insects, worms, birds, mammals, fungi etc.). In a circle, give out a card to each member of the group. Ask: 'What is the source of all energy on the earth?' (The sun). Start by giving the ball of wool to the person holding the 'sun' card. Ask: 'Who depends on the sun for its food?' (A plant). The sun then tosses the ball of wool to the plant whilst holding on to one end. Then continue by asking: 'Who is connected to the plant and can you explain the connection?' and the wool gets passed across the circle until everyone is connected in a web. It is possible for some parts of the ecosystem to be connected several times. Remember connections can be for shelter, building materials, protection etc. as well as food.

When all parts are connected, ask the group to take up any slack in the wool so that the links are more obvious. Introduce a threat to the web, e.g. pollution to water or spraying insecticide and demonstrate the repercussions this could produce on other parts of the web by asking each person to let go of the wool as they become affected or to sit down still holding the wool.

Everything goes somewhere.

> I bequeath myself to the dirt
> To grow for the grass I love
> If you want to see me again
> Look for me under your bootsole.
> Walt Whitman

Everything which happens on the earth—living, eating, growing, dying—happens in the air, water or soil. These basic raw materials are used over and over again. The water we drink has been recycled millions of times. We breathe the same recycled air the dinosaurs breathed. Nutrients from the soil are taken in through the roots of plants and return to the soil once the plant decays. Likewise when we die our ashes cannot disappear but form part of the same nutrient cycle.

As leaders we can use the outdoors to introduce the concept of cycles. For example, there are many opportunities to discuss changes of weather and the

seasons. Throughout the year young people can observe the new growth of
plants in spring and later the flowering, fruiting, seed dispersal and decay
towards the end of the year. The *water cycle* also comes to life in the outdoors.
We can sometimes see the build up of clouds, experience the heavy rain and
see its impact on rivers and waterfalls. Later we may feel the drying effect of
the sun and the wind as water is evaporated back into the atmosphere,
eventually to form more clouds.

We can discuss the *nutrient cycle*. Plants get their nutrients in water from
the soil whereas animals get their nutrients by eating other plants or animals.
Fungi get nutrients by living off dead and sometimes living plants and
animals. Nutrients are returned to the soil through droppings and leaf fall as
well as when plants and animals die. This cycling of nutrients is going on all
around us, we just need to use our eyes to see the signs.

Similarly leaders can introduce *life cycles*. For example, young people can
observe the life cycle of frogs from frog-spawn to tadpoles to adults or the life
cycle of butterflies as they change from caterpillars to pupae to adults. They
can wonder at the mayfly larvae in a stream and realise this animal, at a
particular stage in its cycle, suddenly takes off and flies for its final few hours
before becoming part of the nutrient cycle.

Everything is always changing
Nothing in nature stands still, change is the norm. Some changes occur over
millions of years. The distribution of land, sea, climate and vegetation have
changed dramatically through time. For example, in some geological periods
Europe was covered by shallow tropical seas, at other times by dry, sandy
deserts and at other times by glaciers and ice sheets. The evidence for these
past landscapes is present in the rocks and landforms we see today. For most
of the earth's history there was no life on the planet. When we visit parts of
Britain we can touch rocks which were formed before even the simplest
creatures existed, other rocks show us fossils of animals and plants that have
long since disappeared. Species have adapted over long periods to particular
situations and habitats. Landscapes continue to change. There are few
completely wild, natural landscapes remaining on the earth. Increasingly,
most environments show the signs of human activities.

Species of plants and animals found in a community do not stay the same
forever. For example, if a piece of farmland is abandoned some plants and
animals will take over initially but gradually be replaced by others. This
process is called ecological succession. Some areas of Britain, for example, would eventually
return to deciduous woodland if the grazing of animals was eliminated.

Living things change over long periods of time; they evolve and adapt to
their surroundings. The beaks of birds are a good example of adaptation. For
example, birds of prey have hooked beaks for tearing flesh, waders often have
long beaks for digging deep into sand and mud banks, finches have strong,
broad beaks to crush seeds and nuts and flycatchers thin beaks to catch insects.

Understanding evolution and change can help us to appreciate our own
life. We know that many species have disappeared and our own actions have
placed many others under the threat of extinction.

There is no such thing as a free lunch

Everything we do affects the earth. Consider waking up after a night camping in the mountains. Surely this represents a low-impact activity? We wake up inside our man-made fibre sleeping bags, inside a tent made in Poland, which is another product of the petroleum industry. We pull on a mixture of man-made and natural fibre garments—cotton from India, wool from Scotland, zips from Korea, fleece from ICI of no fixed address. The leather in our boots comes from Italian cows and the rubber is from plantations in Malaysia. We light a stove made from metal which originated in Canada and South America with a match whose wood was once growing in Sweden. Our water is from the local beck but comes with atmospheric particles from three continents. It boils and we pour it into our Chinese plastic mug and onto our teabag which is derived from a plant grown on the steep hillsides of Sri Lanka. We add a little Swiss powdered milk and some sugar that has been squeezed from canes grown on Barbados. We are ready to start preparing breakfast. Our cereal once grew in the USA, the margarine is from vegetable oils derived from Europe and Africa, the bacon is from Danish pigs, salt is from mines in Cheshire and pepper from southern India.

We are now ready to enjoy the outdoors, but first it is worth making a few connections. What happened to the Malaysian tropical rain forest that was replaced by rubber plantations and how many species disappeared with it? What insecticides and fertilisers are applied to the maize crop in the USA and the tea plantations in Sri Lanka and where do these chemicals end up? What about the costs of mechanisation in farming and the transportation of products around the globe? What is their effect on the world's resources?

Outdoor leaders can use many situations in the outdoors to raise questions about our connections with the earth and to illustrate the concept of 'no free lunch'.

Activity—Origins

Consider the impact of a day's outdoor activity. Use the following headings to discuss the impact:

1. Transport to and from the site.
2. Clothing.
3. Food.
4. Equipment.
5. Impact of activity on the site.

For 1–4 make connections with the raw materials used and their place of origin. What are the possible repercussions on environments in other countries?

For 5 try to assess the impact of the group's activity in terms of physical damage, ecological disturbance or nuisance to other people (see chapter 8).

Everything has limits
All of Earth's resources are limited. Some such as the fossil fuels (oil, gas and coal) and minerals are non-renewable. We can use them only once. We have treated resources as if they are limitless and we have become ever dependent on new technology to allow further exploitation. This process has damaged environments and many animals and plants have become extinct. There is now a concerted effort to maintain bio-diversity, the rich variety of life in the world's ecosystems.

Other resources such as trees and agricultural crops are renewable but we need to conserve and replace existing supplies. One of the main problems we face on the earth is that a small proportion of the world's population is consuming most of its resources. We are part of this so-called 'developed world', which is characterised by over consumption and waste. Our lifestyles have led to a loss of bio-diversity in many areas of the world. The rich countries of the north are beginning to realise that they can no longer dump their waste at sea or burn it without repercussions. The earth has a limited capacity to deal with our waste.

In contrast, most of the world's people live by satisfying their basic needs for food, shelter and clothing and millions struggle to find enough resources to stay alive. Both over consumption and extreme poverty lead to environmental degradation.

An understanding of ecology provides us with much more than a factual understanding of biotic relationships. It begs us to question our own attitudes and values to life on this planet. We can begin to look critically at our connections. Environmental education relates ecological understanding to personal and social behaviour.

Critical enquiry

> For most people and most educators, outdoor experience of the natural world, an understanding of ecology and an awareness of environmental issues represent the basics of environmental education. But this approach is severely limited.
>
> Peter Martin (1996)

Peter Martin argues that in educating for sustainability it is not enough to offer direct experience or understand the scientific relationships or even suggest a set of defined attitudes and values. We must provide opportunities for young people to think for themselves and come to their own conclusions. Environmental education is about good education, it is about enabling young people to understand and participate in the democratic process.

Through enquiry we can begin to answer the question: 'How are decisions made which influence environments?' One approach to critical enquiry using the outdoors is through field studies.

Field studies—From eyeballing to enquiry

Most young people are introduced to fieldwork through outdoor teaching related to the geography and biology curricula. In its traditional form it may emphasise looking, seeing and simple recording—the 'eyeball' technique. This can be a useful introduction to a new environment and help to give young people a feel for the landscape or an element of it. But it is often teacher led and may be unstructured.

Some time ago, fieldwork suffered from an ill-founded attempt to be objective and to try to measure everything in sight. Quadrats were thrown at random and plant species painstakingly counted, rivers were analysed using tape measures, clinometers and floating oranges, and young people stood at busy road junctions recording traffic flows until they were bored silly. It was all in the cause of trying to be more scientific. Field studies adopted the scientific method with its sequence of stages as shown in figure 9.1.

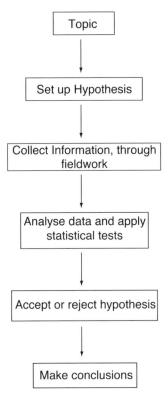

Figure 9.1. Scientific approach to fieldwork

A hypothesis was set up, for example, relating the gradient of a stream to the frequency of meanders or the range of shops in a village to the size of its population. Information was gathered and analysed with statistical tests applied to give credibility. In the end the hypothesis was accepted or rejected and the implications discussed. It was argued that this approach gave structure and rigour to the field studies. But a major concern was its relevance. Did these relationships between river or settlement characteristics matter anyway or was it just an academic exercise? Can we be, or should we even try to be, objective when we are part of the environment we are trying to measure?

Fortunately field studies has changed and has moved away from investigating isolated parts of a physical, biological, social or economic system. The emphasis in environmental fieldwork is now on an understanding of real issues and this involves considering the relationships between human and natural systems. For example, a study of the freshwater ecology of a stream may begin by looking at habitats, life cycles and food chains. It may be extended by considering how the presence or absence of particular species indicates different levels of pollution. If mayfly and stonefly nymphs are present then the water is very clean. If these are absent but caddisfly lava and freshwater shrimps occur then there is slight pollution. With increasing pollution there are water louse and bloodworms. Finally the absence of all of these species and the presence of sludgeworm and rat-tailed maggots indicates a high level of pollution. Such an investigation could lead to a comparison of streams and may raise questions and further study on the causes of the pollution. This is an example of an enquiry approach where young people become actively involved in questions, issues and problems. An outline of this approach is shown in figure 9.2.

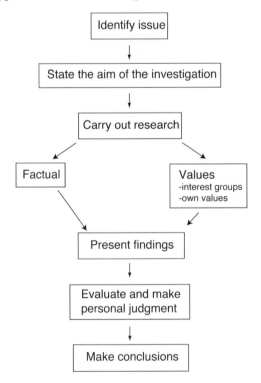

Figure 9.2. Enquiry approach to fieldwork

This approach is far more relevant to education for sustainability since it involves young people in a wide range of skills and allows them to explore other peoples' attitudes and values and develop and clarify their own. They have to select methods to gather factual information and a range of opinions from interest groups, discuss conflict situations, weigh up arguments and make their own judgements. This process helps in their understanding of how decisions are made and should encourage their active participation in issues affecting the environment.

There are many issues with environmental implications that outdoor leaders can use as a basis for an enquiry approach. Here are a few examples, many more can be found from local newspapers:

- The building of a large supermarket on the edge of a town.
- The location of a wind farm.
- The closure of a primary school in a small village.
- Conflicts of interest between conservationists and recreationists over the use of a lake.
- The construction of a large barrage across an estuary.
- The building of a new bypass for a town.
- The impact of second and retirement homes on rural areas.
- The use of ancient trackways by four-wheel-drive vehicles.
- The extension of a quarry in a national park.
- The flooding of a valley for a reservoir.

I have chosen one of these issues, the extension of quarrying in a national park, as a case study to show how an enquiry approach to fieldwork can be used.

Case study—Quarrying in a national park; enquiry-based fieldwork

The issue
The issue is the extension of an existing quarry in a National Park, one of 11 areas of England and Wales designated as a landscape of national importance requiring special protection. The National Park Authority has a duty under the 1995 Environment Act to conserve and enhance the natural beauty, wildlife and cultural heritage and to promote opportunities for the understanding and enjoyment of the special qualities of the Park by the public. It also has responsibility for fostering the social and economic well-being of local communities in the Park. There is a need to strike a balance between conservation, recreation and the local economy.

The aim of the investigation
The aim is to research the issue, weighing up the arguments for and against the extension of the quarry and to reach a judgement on the evidence collected.

Research including fieldwork
This might include:

1. Investigating the history of quarrying on the site. There may be a long tradition of quarrying in the area and the activity may pre-date the establishment of the National Park. Information can be sought from books, old maps and records, local historians etc.
2. Considering the value of quarrying to the local community. How many jobs are provided directly and indirectly? Will the extension create extra employment or protect existing jobs? What alternatives are available? Sources of information may be the company's annual report, articles in newspapers, interviews with local people.
3. Assessing the impact of the quarry extension. There will probably be a visual impact on the landscape in terms of the extended quarry face and the larger spoil heaps. There may be an impact on wildlife and the expansion may lead to greater noise and more quarry traffic on narrow, local roads. Young people can devise their own schemes for landscape assessment and use them as part of their fieldwork. They can also take photos and make sketches and plans to show the existing and proposed developments.
4. Seeking opinions from different interest groups. Examples of this may be interviews or questionnaire surveys of local people and visitors, including people employed in the quarries, parish councillors, members of amenity and conservation groups, etc. Other sources of information may be letters and comments in the local press and radio and from public meetings.
5. Putting the issue into the national context. Is the expansion of quarrying in the national interest? Are there alternative sources of the rock outside the National Park? What are the National Park Authority's policies on such extensions? This kind of information is usually available from National Park reports, policy documents, interviews with officers or the Park's education and information service.

Presenting findings
This research will produce both factual information and the opinions of different interest groups. There are many ways of presenting the ideas. It could be a group report, a presentation to a public meeting in the form of role play or a group may be asked to put forward their views in the form of a short interview for radio or television. Ideas for using drama techniques in issue-based work are described later in this chapter.

Evaluating and making judgements
Young people can be drawn into real issues and they may express their own views according to their interests and values. It is also possible that they may change or adapt their opinions in the light of discussion and debate. It is important that they appreciate that very few issues are clear cut. For example, although many would contend that quarrying detracts from the beauty of the landscape, it nevertheless provides jobs for local people, keeps villages and traditions alive and may help to restrict second home ownership.

Case study—Blue-green algae on Coniston Water; learning through a real issue

The problem
Coniston Water is a beautiful lake within the Lake District National Park. It has for many years been a popular lake for a variety of recreational activities. Today these include sailing, windsurfing, fishing, canoeing and swimming. There are car parks, picnic areas, camping facilities and guest houses around the lake. A 16 kph speed limit on the lake prevents use by power boats and helps maintain a peaceful environment. Planning controls and management plans ensure the conservation of landscape and wildlife around the lake.

In summer 1994 the first signs of blue-green algae appeared on the lake producing concern from local people, lake users and environmentalists. This was an obvious visual sign that natural systems were under stress. One local resident said, 'it looked scary; there was a scum on the water like pea soup with bright blue patches around the edges'. These algal blooms are toxic and can be as poisonous as cobra venom. They can kill fish and other freshwater life and although unlikely to be consumed by humans, may lead to skin rashes, eye irritations, vomiting and diarrhoea (Department of Health—Warning). The presence of blue-green algae could have a marked impact on recreational use of the lake and in so doing affect the tourist trade in general in the Coniston area.

The causes—awareness and understanding
Algal blooms on lakes are caused by the increasing accumulation of nutrients, usually phosphates and nitrates, in the water. Algae deprive fish and other plants of the oxygen, light and space they need to survive. This process is known as eutrophication (see figure 9.3). The two major sources of nitrates and phosphates in Coniston

---

PROCESS OF EUTROPHICATION

Nitrates, phosphates and organic matter from sewage or
farm waste.
⇩
Food for bacteria and algae, which multiply.
⇩
Oxygen removed from water.
⇩
Conditions unsuitable for aquatic life so organisms in lake
die.
⇩
Breakdown of organic matter producing compounds such as
hydrogen sulphide and methane.
⇩
Polluted water unable to support most living organisms.

Figure 9.3.

Water are effluent from the sewage works and run-off and leaching
from agricultural land, silage dumps and slurry stores. Algal
blooms are more common in warm, calm conditions in shallow
water. These conditions were prevalent throughout the hot
summer of 1996.

Taking action

Involvement in a real life issue such as this can lead to good
environmental education. The following questions can be
identified.

- What is happening? This relates to awareness of the issue.
- Why is it happening? This relates to understanding of the issue.
- What does it mean to me and the community? This relates to
  our attitudes and values.
- What can I do? Who can help? This implies action.

Sequence of events

1. Reports of blue-green algae by local lake users made to the
   Coniston Water Safety Meeting.
2. Special meeting called with an expert from the Freshwater
   Biological Station.
3. At the meeting it was decided to:
   (a) Write individual letters to the National Rivers Authority who
   are responsible for ensuring water quality.

(b) Report all further incidents of blue-green algae to the Coniston Boating Centre.
4. First reports of skin irritations appear in the local press.
5. Notices are put up by the National Park Authority warning visitors not to swim in the lake.
6. A system is set up to monitor water quality on Coniston Water by inspector from National Rivers Authority.
7. Community pressure for a phosphate stripper at the sewage plant, Coniston.

Action is continuing.

Activity—Questions for discussion

Consider the above sequence of events. Is this action tackling the root cause?

How could we alleviate the problem through changes in our own personal behaviour?

Compare the use of catalytic converters for cars and phosphate strippers for sewage works.

This raises fundamental questions in educating for sustainable environments.

Case study—Should the Upper Duddon be flooded? Exploring an issue through writing and role play

Terry Gifford, the poet and environmentalist mentioned earlier, runs writers' workshops for young people in the Duddon Valley in Cumbria. He uses issues, such as 'Should the Upper Duddon Valley be flooded to meet our growing needs for water?' as the focus and stimulus for writing. His groups use the outdoors to consider the effects of flooding on the environment and they assess the views of local people on the proposed development. They are asked to support or oppose the proposal and they use writing and role play to express their feelings and ideas.

Here are some of the ideas that Terry uses:

1. Divide the young people into groups of about five or six. Some will support the proposal others will oppose it.

2. Groups collect 'evidence' which are mainly forms of writing from their guided exercises, most written outdoors.
3. There is a final presentation on the last day and each group can use several different forms of work to persuade the others.
4. Finally there is a free vote with ballot papers, an introduction to electoral voting.

Young people produce different forms of poetry, based on the work of Terry and other poets. Here is a poem, jointly written, that captures the special elements of the Duddon Valley at night.

In the Night in Dunnerdale

The stars were like balls of fire spirits
Running across deep velvet

The wall was like feeling a mouth
With giants' teeth in it

The mountains looked like gods
Watching over us

The wind was like giants
Blowing gently on us

The tree was like a hand
Reaching out to grab the earth
And pull it down

The grass was like friendly hands
Showing us the way to go

The forest darkness is like being trapped
In a dream,
A wild dream,
Not scary,
But splendid

The lights of Hinning House
Were like glow worms frozen in giant ice cubes.

Helen Nuttall and Emma Tickle

As part of their presentation they can report on interviews they make with four valley residents- a teenager, a ranger, a shop owner and a farmer. These locals are role-played by leaders. There is also the chance to present their ideas in the form of a play or poster.

The value of drama

Like outdoor education, drama is concerned with active and experiential methods of learning. Although it does not concentrate on the acquisition of knowledge, drama requires research skills and often motivates learning. It is perhaps more important as a way of enabling people to discover their own feelings and clarify their values.

There are many routes to understanding. Drama is less conventional, it has freshness, it appeals to our creative side and may lead to deeper levels of understanding. Drama recognises that everyone has a wealth of knowledge and experience and that this needs to be tapped. Sometimes it can demonstrate that people know more than they thought, a concept referred to as 'metacognition'. This has clear links with education for sustainability where we are trying to empower young people.

Drama is a social activity and for many young people this in itself encourages motivation and learning. By working together to create drama people develop many interpersonal skills. They learn to negotiate, compromise and work as a member of a team. But drama can also be very personal and encourage reflection and challenge our attitudes and values.

Drama draws on real-life situations and can be a powerful way of exploring environmental issues. It offers young people the opportunity to examine a situation from another person's point of view. For further discussion on the use of drama in education see Wagner (1979), Morgan and Saxton (1987), O'Toole (1992) and Heathcote and Bolton (1995). This case study concentrates on how drama can be used in outdoor education to bring an environmental issue alive.

Case study—A cable car up Coniston Old Man? Exploring an issue through drama

Introducing the issue
The leader introduces the idea of a proposal to construct a cable car up a popular mountain in the National Park and suggests that different members of the local community may have different views on such a development.

Assigning roles
Members of the group are assigned to a variety of roles in the community. Examples could be: a local farmer; a young mother; a shopkeeper; a retired person; a member of the Mountain Rescue team; a taxi driver; a second home owner; a publican; a quarry worker; a lorry driver; a naturalist; a mountain walker. Role cards can be used to give more information and help the individual empathise with the character. For example, here are two possible characters:

Dan Baxter came to the village on retirement after working for many years in the city. He chose the place because it was less developed than many other villages. He enjoys gardening, playing bowls and meeting his friends for a pint at the local pub. He likes the village as it is and thinks that a cable car will attract more tourists, noise and extra traffic on the roads.

Dorothy Page is the local taxi driver who has lived in the village all her life. She struggles to make a living from her small business and takes on extra cleaning jobs to supplement her income. She is a popular figure in the community and helps to organise social events for elderly people as well as delivering shopping to some of them each week. She welcomes the cable car as it will bring jobs to the village and more demand for her taxi service.

Stepping into the person's shoes
Individuals, or partners if it is a large group, try to get a feeling for their assigned character. They gather information about the issue from the standpoint of the particular person. Some of this information can be gained by visiting the village and making a journey up the mountain. Old and present-day photos and maps, past accounts of industry and recent management plans, letters to the local press (real or imaginary) will provide other useful evidence in making a case.

The case for the cable car
The leader takes on the role of the spokesperson for the development. The case is presented at a public meeting held in the village which is attended by the various characters suggested earlier. The representative's proposal might take the following form:

'The Coniston Cable Car Company have plans to build the first cable car up a mountain in England. It will provide an opportunity for all kinds of people to enjoy the mountains. The young, elderly and physically disabled will be able to experience the views from the top of the mountain. The proposal is to construct the cable car from Coniston village to the top of The Old Man, the most popular summit in the district. The summit already receives thousands of visitors each year and the top is heavily eroded. The mountain has had a long industrial heritage especially related to copper mining and slate quarrying. In the past there were many overhead cableways and there are numerous spoil heaps from the mines and quarries visible today. There is still a large working slate quarry on the side of the mountain facing the village. A modern, quiet cable car system will enhance rather than detract from a landscape that has been heavily influenced by human activities. The cable car will create new jobs in the area and help to support some of the existing tourist businesses. It can also be argued that it will take pressure off the overused paths, help to protect some plant species and could be used by the Mountain Rescue team in emergencies'.

Responding in role
The characters in the audience respond to this presentation by questioning the company's spokesperson and stating their own point of view on the pros and cons of the development. Following the meeting this could be extended further by the technique known as 'hot seating'. Each character is put under the spotlight and takes it in turns to answer questions from the rest of the group. This helps the individual to gain a deeper appreciation of the person they are portraying.

Follow-up
Groups of those in favour or those opposed to the building of the cable car come together and are asked to work on a project. Some examples might be:

1. Prepare for a three-minute interview to put across their case on local radio. A member of the group could be asked to play the role of interviewer.
2. Design a poster or leaflet to put forward their arguments.
3. Use the technique of 'still image' or 'tableau' to show the consequences of the development. Using their bodies groups create a scene or incident which is captured or frozen at one point in time, like a photograph. It is also possible to allow the 'still image' to come to life, with actions and even speech. The interpretation of the 'still image' by the observers is as important a part of the process as creating the photograph itself.

    An extension of this idea is to invite the groups making the 'still images' to work in a more symbolic or abstract form asking them to respond to a word such as 'exploitation' for their image making.
4. Ask individuals to do a short piece of writing in role. This could take the form of a diary entry from a person affected by the plans in some way; a Cable Car Company memo about the development; or a press report in the style of a local newspaper, a tabloid newspaper or an environmental journal. This type of writing encourages young people to make personal reflections on the issues and to consider different viewpoints, bias and the way language is used in the media.

In contrast, the following case study uses a drama approach to explore environmental concepts through personal and group reflection rather than through a conflict of issues.

Case study—The allotment

Phil Sixsmith, a drama specialist, and Elissavet Tsaliki, an environmental educationist have created a drama in education workshop based on the 'allotment' and the concept of sustainable living. This is especially useful for outdoor leaders working with groups in the urban environment.

Phil and Elissavet use an approach known as the 'Mantle of the Expert', which was originated by the British drama educator, Dorothy Heathcote. In this approach, young people become the experts, leading the process and helping to solve the problems even though they know they are only participating in a fiction.

Here are some of the steps, based on Phil and Elissavet's work, which can be used in investigating this aspect of urban living:

1. Introduce the idea of an allotment. The Concise Oxford Dictionary defines it as 'apportioning; lot in life; share alloted to one; small portion of land let out for cultivation'. Through discussion agree a definition of allotment that suits everyone, for example, ' a small piece of land in a town used mainly for the cultivation of vegetables for the owner's personal consumption'.
2. Ask each young person to choose a partner and from their own experiences describe their image of an allotment. What does it look like? What words encapsulate their allotment? Paint a word picture for each other. For example, my allotment is: 'a haven, it is cared for, it is close to a railway line, it is an escape, there are sheds, onions, leeks, competitions'. For groups with limited experience, they could visit one or two nearby allotments at this stage and chat to a few owners. If this is not possible a few photographs may help to give them ideas.
3. The leader presents the group with a personal opinion:

'My allotment represents a step towards sustainable living'.

This is written in the centre of a large sheet of paper and put on a wall. Without discussion, the leader asks: ' I wonder if you, as fellow allotment holders could find a statement or image which supports this belief'. At this point the young people begin to enrol in the drama, they begin to express their personal thoughts and feelings, adding them to the sheet of paper.

4. Participants are asked to focus on one of the drawn images or written statements and imagine themselves on their piece of land. They create still images of themselves busy at some task on their allotment. These images are brought to life and individuals asked to speak their thoughts out loud, at first all together, letting the thoughts fill the allotment and then, if they wish, out loud for all to hear when tapped on the shoulder. Individuals may be involved in smelling the earth, breaking up the soil, raking, digging, resting in their deck chair etc., some may even have actual childhood memories of a particular allotment.

5. A letter arrives from BBC World Service Television. The facilitator, in role as an allotment owner, reads out the letter which states that BBC World are making a documentary programme on 'Sustainable Systems' and request assistance from experienced allotment owners (participants in role). If the group is interested a representative will call to discuss the programme. This raises interest and excitement in the group and they discuss how they will respond. They decide whether to co-operate and try to assess the potential problems. If they go ahead they need to decide how to reply, what aspects they wish to present and how to negotiate a contract. They may need to consider how their allotment is sustainable and whether there are any issues such as the use of chemical fertilisers. Small groups can work on these considerations.

6. Before making their final decisions on the TV programme the group may wish to research the links between sustainability and allotments by visiting a local allotment and interviewing owners. This may involve the group in designing a suitable questionnaire, recording and presenting their findings.

With the exception of 'The Allotment' most of the case studies outlined above are based on issues I am familar with in my local area. Issues are all around us in the outdoors and the methods suggested in this section using enquiry based field studies, writing and drama can be applied to any number of other situations.

10. Action

Action speaks louder than words

The role of leaders in setting a personal example should not be underestimated. I have argued in chapter three that outdoor leaders have many advantages over, for example, school teachers and as a result they can be powerful role models. If the leader is seen as macho, competitive and insensitive to people and to the environment then this is likely to adversely influence the group's attitudes and behaviour. The leader who offers fun and excitement but who also cares for the group and inspires an interest in the environment can have a significant impact on an individual's development.

Young people are perceptive to the leader's actions. If the leader talks of the benefits of using public transport or cycling but rolls up each day in a large, noisy car, this inconsistency will not be lost on the group. Similarly the leader who professes to be interested in empowering young people by giving them responsibility but who talks too much and continually interferes in their learning will also be obvious. The 'media', the actions of the leader, must match the message.

Young people are perceptive to the leader's actions, for example travel to work.

Small actions by the leader may be more powerful than a thousand words. The leader who, after an exciting rock scramble, stops to watch a bird circle overhead or stoops down to smell a flower, may present an image which confronts a young person's values or triggers their curiosity. A leader picking up litter from a lakeshore and putting it in their bag without comment may provoke questions from individuals and provide a much stronger message than any amount of talking about litter collection.

If we are interested in educating for more sustainable lifestyles it is important that we improve our own actions and encourage young people to consider their actions. The following Activity may help as a starting point for this discussion. It can be used by the leader to assess his or her own actions prior to use with a group of young people.

Activity—Towards sustainability. What can I do?

Here are 25 suggestions:

- Get to know my local environment
- Walk instead of using the car
- Use my local shops
- Plant a tree
- When writing use both sides of the paper
- Save and recycle glass and cans
- Tell other people about what I like in the area
- Avoid buying over-packaged things
- Do not leave the tap running when I am cleaning my teeth
- Watch a bird closely or smell a wildflower
- Turn the heating down and put on a jumper
- Find out where my clothes were made
- Cycle in the countryside
- Discover a building I like in the town
- Buy goods from abroad that have been traded fairly
- Join a local club
- Write a letter to the paper on something I feel strongly about
- Help an old person in my community
- Support a charity that works to help poor people
- Put food out for birds in winter
- Turn off lights when not in use
- Start a compost bin
- Find my own special place to spend time in the outdoors
- Get to know my neighbour better
- Watch a sunrise or a sunset.

Which of these relate to conservation, social or economic considerations?

Which are related to local, national orglobal considerations?

Brainstorm another 25 personal actions to add to the list.

Your organisation—Asking the questions

As well as considering our personal actions, it is also important to look at our organisation and the programmes we offer. Asking questions in our organisation is not always an easy task. The outdoor leader may be a small voice in a large organisation. The structures may be imposed from outside, such as through a local authority which determines pay scales, conditions of service, working practices, health and safety standards, etc. The aims of the

organisation may also be quite different from the leader wishing to introduce sustainable ideas and practices. Some organisations exist on a commercial basis, as part of the leisure industry. Their aims may be to offer a wide range of recreational activities to as many young people as possible, giving them exciting experiences and hoping they will return for more. Other organisations may have an educational remit but this might be seen in terms of the development of physical or sports skills. Some organisations will have personal, social and environmental education as their aims and these probably offer the easiest opportunities for change.

As a starting point it is essential to see how your aims for environmental awareness and sustainability fit into the overall goals of your organisation. You will need to clarify three questions:

1. What are the aims of the organisation?
2. What are the needs of the young people?
3. What are my aims as a leader?

There may be a conflict between these sets of aims which will usually be resolved by some form of compromise. It might mean that the leader who is interested in educating for sustainability has to assess what can realistically be achieved within his/her organisation.

Even if the management of your organisation is interested in environmental education it could be for a variety of reasons. For example, introducing environmental activities might take pressure off staffing more intensive ones, such as climbing or kayaking; it might be good for public relations; it might be a way of raising extra income or it might be to meet the requirements of the school or youth service curriculum. These reasons may be quite different from your own beliefs in trying to encourage more sustainable lifestyles. They may influence what you can achieve.

On the other hand you may be in a situation where you can have a strong influence on the organisation or where you have considerable independence in the way you operate. In these cases you should achieve more substantial changes.

Greening the organisation

There is a generally accepted process in planning for change in any organisation. It can be summarised as follows:

1. Start with an audit or review of current practice. This will involve looking at the whole organisation, all the staff and the work it undertakes with young people.
2. Decide what changes you wish to make as a result of the audit. Draw up a list of priorities and a plan for action.
3. Put forward a policy for environmental education and sustainability. Involve young people in drawing up this policy.
4. Implement the policy and action plan.
5. Evaluate its success over a specified period of time. Review and update action plans.

When considering an audit related to good environmental and sustainable practice it is important to realise we are interested in much more than collecting litter, recycling cans and saving energy. The philosophy should permeate the whole life of the organisation, the attitudes and behaviour of the staff and their work with young people. The following guidelines may make this clearer:

• The aim should be holistic education. Personal, social and environmental awareness and skills are all part of the same process. This ethos should permeate the work of the organisation.
• Organisations should move away from narrow programmes based on academic fieldwork or outdoor pursuits. They should broaden their base to

include other approaches, for example, through art, drama or problem solving, which encourage environmental learning.

- Organisations should question the importance they place on activities. Are they an end in themselves or used as a vehicle for learning? Are there opportunities to 'plan, do and review'?
- Organisations should develop programmes in consultation with young people to give a sense of ownership and self-reliance. The ethos of the organisation should be conducive to this process.
- Teaching and learning styles should be varied and flexible depending on activities and situations. They should be designed to encourage all young people to achieve their potential. Leaders can help to 'unlock talent' which has failed to emerge through formal education.
- Organisations should address all aspects of environmental education from awareness, understanding and the development of skills to the discussion of attitudes and values and the ways in which action can be taken. They should tackle the major ecological concepts which govern all life on the planet. Through environmental issues they should also introduce economic and political systems and how they influence the environment. The aim should be to develop citizens who are environmentally competent and who wish to live more sustainably.
- Organisations should have an 'open' policy fostering links with the local community and other organisations and agencies working towards similar aims. They should look at ways of sharing expertise with other organisations and encourage in-service development of their own staff.
- Organisations should try to improve their own environmental actions for instance in terms of energy saving, recycling and use of materials. They should examine their activities and use of sites and ensure these are compatible with their overall aims. There should be attempts to improve environments through practical conservation.
- Through their own example, organisations should discuss with leaders and young people ways to make improvements in their own actions and encourage them to adopt more sustainable lifestyles.
- Organisations should try to relate local issues to global patterns. This message should be positive, forward-looking and attempt to broaden horizons and foster international understanding.

These guidelines present a challenge to organisations. Figure 10.1 shows leaders the main aspects of their organisations they will need to consider in their audits. Some of these elements are considered in the following section.

Designing programmes

One starting point is to assess the level of involvement in environmental education and sustainability offered by your existing programme. Try the following activity.

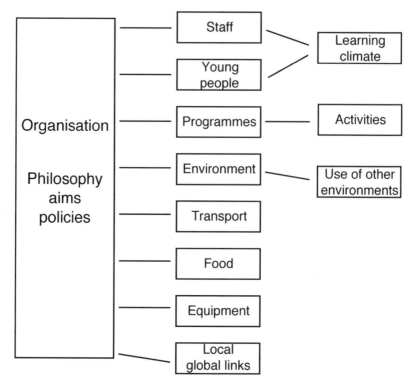

Figure 10.1. Elements to consider in an audit of an organisation

Activity—Level of involvement

Using the ten questions given below, discuss with colleagues your level of involvement in environmental education. You should consider what you are currently doing and what you would like to achieve in the future. In general the actions near the top of the list will be easier to achieve and those near the bottom will require stronger commitment from leaders and the support of their organisations. The list is not a step-by-step sequence but it will give an indication of your level of involvement.
In your programme do you?

- Encourage young people to experience and enjoy a range of environments?
- Develop personal and social skills essential for environmental education?
- Discuss conservation issues and question the impact of your activities with groups?
- Offer activities to encourage sensory awareness?

- Introduce ecological concepts and relate them to ourselves?
- Question social, economic and political attitudes to the environment?
- Take part in practical conservation?
- Link your work to an environmental policy?
- Relate your work to local sustainability and global issues?
- Offer fully integrated programmes of environmental education?

This Activity may help to put your work into perspective. Most outdoor leaders offer programmes which encourage personal and social development and environmental awareness, all of which provides a sound basis for environmental education. Some will go further and introduce key ecological concepts. Fewer leaders will question society's attitudes to the environment and relate their work to local sustainability and global issues. Very few will offer integrated programmes?

Examples of integrated programmes

Outdoor activity programmes are often presented as a series of taster sessions with few connections between each session. Young people may enjoy these sessions but the educational potential is limited. Fieldwork also is sometimes presented as isolated tasks with little cohesion. Exceptions to this are outdoor programmes geared towards training in particular skills where there is a progression from simple to more complex skills often in accordance with nationally recognised training schemes and awards. Similarly some field studies programmes may be project based or related to the needs of the National Curriculum and will, therefore, follow a structure.

The value of integrated programmes is that they provide a focus for learning and are structured towards a definite outcome. There is a theme, sequence and progression to the programme. Integrated outdoor programmes which emphasise environmental education are not common and it is often difficult for leaders who are not centre based to develop such programmes.

The Institute of Earth Education, an organisation based in the United States but with international links, has for many years been developing programmes to encourage young people to 'live more lightly on the earth'. Their tightly structured programmes are based on encouraging feelings for nature, developing ecological understanding and changing personal behaviour. They offer all the key elements of environmental education, from awareness to action, in an exciting package of active outdoor learning experiences. About 12 outdoor organisations in the United Kingdom offer the 'Earthkeepers' programme, which is designed for 10–11 year olds. The most recent programme 'Sunship III' (1997) has been developed for the 13–14 years age group.

Many outdoor leaders will be familiar with the work of the Institute through Steve van Matre's books and training workshops held each year. Some of their activities, such as the sensory walks known as 'Earthwalks', are used extensively. The use of the Institute's extended programmes is more problematic as they require the making of specific props for the activities and need high levels of staffing. Some leaders also find the programmes too prescriptive and leader-dependent and argue that they do not encourage discussion and critical thinking.

The leaders at Gortatole Outdoor Education Centre in County Fermanagh, Northern Ireland, have developed several outdoor programmes that combine adventure and environmental education. One of these 'The Lost Chronicles of Ethar' involves young people journeying to different parts of the planet Ethar to discover and record aspects of the landscape, solve riddles and take action for the environment through a conservation task. There are elements of theatre and role play in the programme. There is an airlock with sound effects and flashing lights to simulate time travel. At each site the group meets shadowy figures who are representatives of each landscape—cave, cliff, mountain, forest, lake and river. These characters help to answer the group's questions concerning the significance of each environment and the threats it faces.

Nottinghamshire education authority has developed a comprehensive programme, 'Trailblazer', for environmental education in its schools. The scheme is supported by two outdoor residential centres and four-day visit centres. Records of achievement are kept for young people and related to the following four strands:

1. field studies
2. outdoor pursuits, safety and survival
3. service to the environment
4. personal and social education

According to Pippa Manson and David Armstrong (1997) of Nottinghamshire's Environmental Education Support Service, 'Trailblazer' encourages young people to become independent learners by promoting direct involvement in setting targets and reviewing experiences. It emphasises the 'plan, do, review' process whilst undertaking environmental activities. Each participant has a 'Trailblazer' record book or file which is used to record experiences, achievements and credits towards the award. Each year there is a special award ceremony for young people who have attained the different levels in the scheme.

One way of leaders creating environmental programmes for their groups is to make use of an existing national award scheme. An example is that offered by the John Muir Trust, an organisation established in1983 and named after the Scot's born founder of the conservation movement in North America. The Trust aims to take practical action to safeguard and protect examples of our wilder and more remote landscapes and at present it owns and manages four extensive areas in Scotland. But it is also interested in encouraging young people to become aware of environments, both locally and further afield, and to help to protect and conserve them. The Trust carried out a survey in 1995 of young people's involvement with environmental groups in Scotland and found that less than 0.1% of the 12–24 years age group are active members of such groups. For most youth organisations environmental projects and award schemes were of low priority. One of the key reasons was that 'most youth leaders lacked the knowledge, skills, experience and confidence to develop or lead an environmental programme with young people'. As a result the Trust has developed training workshops for leaders and environmental awards at three levels for young people.

John Muir Awards

Discovery Award: Entry Level (Minimum 15 hours over 3 months).
Explorer Award: Intermediate (Minimum 30 hours over 6 months).
Conserver Award: Advanced (Minimum 60 hours over 12 months).

Each level of the Award asks for progressively greater effort and commitment and repeats the same four challenges:

1. *Discover a wild place*. This can be a relatively natural area from the back garden, a local park, river or pond to a nature reserve. Plan a programme of visits and keep a record of your experiences.
2. *Explore its wildness*. Explore and study the wild place. What plants and animals live here? Why do they live together? How do they depend on each other? Make a map, collect historical information, take photographs, do a wildlife survey, paint, draw or keep a nature diary.
3. *Take responsibility for protecting it*. What are the threats to the wild area? How can I help to conserve the area? Examples might be: litter collection/clean up; planting trees, shrubs, wild flowers; providing nest boxes and bat boxes; raising funds; writing letters and campaigning.
4. *Share the knowledge and experience you have gained*. Share and celebrate your wild place through an exhibition of photographs, paintings, drawings or words; make a video; give a slide show or lead a guided walk.

The John Muir Award scheme could give valuable support to hundreds of youth workers who regularly use the outdoors for adventure but who wish to involve their groups in more environmental activities. They are not always in a position where they can devise their own environmental programmes.

Leaders working in field study and outdoor education centres are in a stronger position as they have a base with resources and can usually offer intensive residential courses.

Peter Higgins (1997) has suggested that when we are planning programmes we should involve young people in choices but in such a way that they can appreciate the consequences of their decisions. He proposes an approach based on the use of 'carbon credits', where participants are allocated a number of credits at the beginning of a day or week and are asked to make choices, sometimes individually and sometimes as a member of a group. For example, as an individual they may decide to use less credits by taking a shower rather than a bath, or choosing to eat less meat. Groups will be faced with decisions in their use of minibus transport, which is expensive in terms of carbon credits, and their choice of activities. Some activities, such as practical conservation, may earn the group credits whilst other activities dependent on specialist equipment and which may have a heavy impact on the environment, such as mountain biking, will require a lot of credits. The Institute of Earth Education's programme, 'Sunship III', mentioned earlier, also uses a system of credits, called 'solarians', but these are only related to personal choices and do not involve the group in decision making.

These examples should give leaders useful ideas on how to offer more than just isolated, unrelated activities. It is important that we help young people make connections between their lifestyles, the environment and other people on the planet. Well-structured environmental programmes are one way to start this process.

Evaluating activities

Young people often perceive activities as an end in themselves. They are the fun bit of the programme. For leisure providers they will also be the key to success and they will sometimes pack in as many activities as possible to maintain the level of excitement. The outdoor education leader usually takes a different approach and will be working within a framework, which will include the organisation's and the leader's own aims and will organise a programme of learning to meet particular learning outcomes. The activities may not be important in themselves but as a vehicle for encouraging personal, social and environmental awareness and understanding (see figure 10.2). As a result some activities may lend themselves readily to meet these needs, whilst others may be inappropriate or even work against what is trying to be achieved.

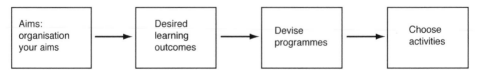

Figure 10.2. Relating activities to aims

Activity—Evaluating activities

This activity is based on the ten essential competencies for sustainability introduced earlier (see chapter one). If we accept these as our desired learning outcomes then it is possible to assess the potential of a selection of outdoor activities in achieving these outcomes. With colleagues use figure 10.3 to evaluate each activity. You can score potential from 0 (no potential) to 5 (great potential). For example you may decide, after discussion, that orienteering has a high potential in terms of co-operation and trust but is low in terms of encouraging a personal response to the environment. The potential of a sensory or earthwalk may be high in terms of developing feelings for the natural environment but low in terms of critical thinking and problem solving.

Your decisions may produce some interesting results. Some activities clearly have a greater potential to meet the required competencies. For example, experiences such as mountain walks, camps and solos may elicit a large range of skills. Others such as abseiling and windsurfing may be very limited for these particular educational aims. In fact it could be argued that abseiling, which places the leader in a dominant role as the instructor and emphasises reliance on equipment and a quick thrill, may actually work against your overall philosophy.

Your completed grid will show you the competencies that are achieved most readily. All the activities should, for example, encourage self-esteem, confidence and motivation. Only a few may be useful in developing critical and futures thinking. The grid may help when planning to incorporate a range of activities in a programme. It may also suggest that there is a need to develop other activities to meet all the required skills.

But this exercise should be treated with care, it is meant only to provoke discussion. We need to remember that the educational potential lies not in the activity *per se* but in the way it is introduced and facilitated by the leader. It is possible, for example, to organise a kayaking session to encourage personal skills and self-reliance or a very different session which emphasises trust and group co-operation. The leader's role will be extremely important and may determine the level of enthusiasm and motivation in the group, how individuals co-operate or compete, how they relate to the environment and how they reflect on their experience. The exercise assumes that the leaders are enthusiastic, democratic and sensitive to the needs of the group and the environment. The grid helps us to consider and question the value of activities we sometimes take for granted.

Figure 10.3. Educational potential of a selection of outdoor experiences

Learning outcomes	Kayaking	Open canoeing	Wind-surfing	Orient-eering	Mountain walking	Self-led walk	Rock scrambling	Abseiling	Camping	Team challenge	Solo	Earth walk	Land art/ nature sculpture	Pond dipping/ river measure-ments	Village study
1 Self-esteem, confidence, motivation															
2 Co-operation, trust, empathy															
3 Communication skills															
4 Critical thinking, problem solving															
5 Self-reliance															
6 Futures thinking															
7 Feelings for natural world															
8 Creativity, personal response to environment															
9 Knowledge of ecology, social/political systems															
10 Reflection and evaluation															

Grade on a 6 point scale: 0 = no potential; 5 = great potential.

Practical conservation—Putting something back

Practical conservation is a physical way of getting young people involved in environmental action and putting something back by protecting or enhancing an environment. It can also help to develop good community relations and lead to useful contacts for the group. There is great potential for leaders to include conservation projects in their programmes. They do not have to be experts as there are plenty of organisations which can give advice.

There are many examples of conservation projects including footpath repair, stonewalling, coppicing, tree and hedge planting, establishing ponds and wetland areas, fencing and putting up nest and bat boxes. Projects need to be chosen with care to match the ability and interests of your group. It is important that young people understand the relevance of the project. For example, cutting back or pulling out bracken or rhododendron for hours may seem a pointless exercise. If possible relate the group's work to their own use of the environment. There may be a small site in their own neighbourhood that the group could adopt and visit on a regular basis, keeping it clean and replanting it.

In upland Britain some conservation issues are produced by the visitors themselves. Footpath erosion is an obvious example, and sometimes a little knowledge can help solve a problem:

> We came across a track in the Little Langdale valley that had been widened as visitors had tried to avoid a badly drained section. The problem had been produced by a blocked culvert under the path. In this case it took the group just ten minutes to clear it. Many leaders had trodden the track and avoided the wet area, unaware that with a little understanding they could have rectified the damage and at the same time involved the group in some sound practical conservation. Later the same group spent two hours repairing a broken stone culvert under another heavily used track. It was a satisfying task, the group felt a real sense of achievement. Several walkers stopped during the afternoon to ask what the group were doing and it seemed clear that many leaders would be prepared to tackle simple repair and maintenance tasks once their eyes had been opened.

Another example of involving a group in a real issue relates to canoeing:

> The group discussed the damage to the river banks at a popular access point for canoeists. Local knowledge had shown that it was clearly the most appropriate launching site and there was little to be gained from trying to direct canoeists elsewhere. The solution was straightforward; the group constructed a hard standing which is now used by most canoeists and this has contained the wear and tear along the river bank.

The key to setting up conservation projects in your local area or one you are visiting is to contact organisations such as the British Trust for Conservation Volunteers, Groundwork (see the Useful Addresses section) or the local ranger service. They will put you in touch with existing projects that you could try out with your group before developing your own schemes.

Making wider links

It is an opportune time for leaders who are interested in environmental education and sustainability. Local governments across the United Kingdom are developing strategies for Local Agenda 21s and many have appointed officers to co-ordinate their programmes. Agenda 21, the global plan for sustainable development, states that the involvement of young people is essential for our future. National organisations like Rescue Mission UK and the Council for Environmental Education are helping to develop a Youth Action 21 and local youth forums are being established. These can give young people opportunities to express their views and help to empower them to take action for their local community and environment. Leaders can act as a catalyst in this process.

We are also fortunate in Britain in having many non-governmental organisations interested in the environment. Some of these, such as Friends of the Earth, act as pressure groups to improve environments and the quality of life. Others may be concerned with protecting particular aspects of the natural or built environment. These groups are beginning to make networks and alliances and they produce a wide range of educational materials and guidance for leaders. Conservation groups, wildlife trusts, city farms, Groundwork trusts and ranger services may be able to offer local support and advice.

Alan Dearling and Howie Armstrong (1997) in their recent book, *Youth Action and Environment* suggest many ways in which young people can get involved in local environmental projects. Their approach is both unusual and refreshing. They do not confine themselves to the easy issues of litter collection and recycling but introduce a much more thought provoking range of issues including ideas from young people involved in road and tree protest campaigns. Like the authors, I believe it is important for young people to discuss the value of all forms of action for the environment.

The message to leaders is clear; try to take advantage of this wealth of information and support and make connections between your environmental work and the bigger picture. Acting locally is an excellent starting point. It will lead into a consideration of national issues and in turn will help us to appreciate that we are all part of a global system.

References and further reading

Anderson, P. (1990). *Moorland Recreation and Wildlife in the Peak District*, Peak Park Joint Planning Board

Andras, V. (1991). The School Subject Bases of Environmental Education in Hungary in *Environmental Education and the Teaching of Biology in Hungary 1970–90*, IUCN Committee on Education in Hungary

Barrett, J.,and Greenaway, R. (1995). *Why Adventure?* Foundation for Outdoor Adventure, Coventry

Beasley, F. (1997). *A Study of the Recreational Impact of Gill Use within the Lake District National Park*, student dissertation

Bowers, C. (1990). Educational computing and the ecological crisis: Some questions about our curriculum priorities, *Journal of Curriculum Studies*, 22

British Mountaineering Council (1988). *Tread Lightly*, British Mountaineering Council

Bunce, R. (1983). Is climbing killing off Lakeland's plant life? *Lakescene Magazine*, Dec. 1983

Burns, S., and Lamont, G. (1995). *Values and Visions—A Handbook for Spiritual Development and Global Awareness*, Hodder and Stoughton

Cooper, G. (Ed.) (1988). *Approaches to the Environment—Towards a Common Understanding*, Adventure and Environmental Awareness Group

Cooper, G. (1994). The role of outdoor education in education for the 21st. century, *Environmental Education*, Summer 1994

Cornell, J. (1979). *Sharing Nature with Children*, Exley

Cornell, J. (1989). *Sharing the Joy of Nature*, Dawn Publications

Dartington Amenity Research Trust (1980). *Groups in the Countryside*, Countryside Commission

Dearling, A. and Armstrong, H. (1997). *Youth Action and the Environment*, Russell House

Dennison, W., and Kirk, R. (1990). *Do, Review, Learn, Apply: A Simple Guide to Experiential Learning*, Blackwell

Déri, A., and Cooper, G. (Eds.) (1993). *Environmental Education—An Active Approach*, Regional Environmental Center for Central and Eastern Europe

Dewey, J. (1938). *Experience and Education*, Collier

Drasdo, H. (1972). *Education and the Mountain Centres*, Tyddyn Gabriel

EDET Group (1992). *Good Earthkeeping—Education, Training and Awareness for a Sustainable Future*, UNEP(UK)

Fuchs, R. H. (1986). *Richard Long*, Thames and Hudson

Gardner, H. (1983). *Frames of Mind: The Theory of Multiple Intelligences*, Palladin

Gifford, T. (1991). *Outcrops*, Littlewood Arc

Gifford, T. (1996). *The Rope*, Redbeck Press

Gittins, J. (1990). *Young People, Adventure and the Countryside*, Countryside Recreation Research Advisory Group, Annual Conference

Goldsworthy A. (1990). *Andy Goldsworthy*, Viking

Goldsworthy A. (1994). *Stone*, Viking

Gregorc, A. (1982). *An Adult's Guide to Style*, Gabriel Systems Inc.

Greig, S., Pike, G., and Selby, D. (1987). *Earthrights—Education as if the Planet Really Mattered*, WWF and Kogan Page Ltd

Heathcote D., and Bolton G. (1995). *Drama for Learning*, Heinman

Heider, J. (1986). *The Tao of Leadership*, Wildwood House Ltd

Henley, T. (1989). *Rediscovery: Ancient Pathways—New Directions*, Western Canada Wilderness Committee

Higgins, P. (1996). Connection and consequence in outdoor education, *Journal of Adventure Education and Outdoor Leadership*, 13 (2)

Higgins, P. (1997). Outdoor education for sustainability: Making connections, *Journal of Adventure Education and Outdoor Leadership*, 13 (3)

Higgins, P., Loynes, C., and Crowther, N. (Eds.) (1997). *A Guide for Outdoor Educators in Scotland*, Adventure Education

Hogan, R. (1992). The natural environment in wilderness programmes—playing field or sacred space? *Journal of Adventure Education and Outdoor Leadership*, 9 (1)

Hopkins, D., and Putnam, R. (1993). *Personal Growth Through Adventure*, David Fulton

Huckle, J. and Sterling, S. (Eds.) (1996). *Education for Sustainability*, Earthscan

Hunt, Lord (Ed.) (1989). *In Search of Adventure: A Study of Opportunities for Adventure and Challenge for Young People*, Talbot Adair Press

Jickling, B. (1992). Why I don't want my children to be educated for sustainable development, *Journal of Environmental Education*, 23 (4)

Joicey, H. B. (1986). *An Eye on the Environment—An Art Education Project*, Bell and Hyman Ltd

Keighley, P. (1997). *The Impact of Experiences Out-of-doors on Personal Development and Environmental Attitudes*, *Journal of Adventure Education and Outdoor Leadership*, 14 (1)

Knowles, J. G. (1992). Geopiety, the concept of Sacred Place: Reflections on an outdoor education experience, *Journal of Experiential Education*, 15 (1)

Liedloff, J. (1989). *The Continuum Concept*, Arkana

Loynes C. (1996). Adventure in a bun, *Journal of Adventure Education and Outdoor Leadership*, 13 (2)

MacLellan, G. (1995). *Talking to the Earth*, Capall Bann

Manson, P., and Armstrong, D. (1997). Environmental education in Nottinghamshire, *Environmental Education*, 56

Mortlock, C. (1984). *The Adventure Alternative*, Cicerone Press

Morgan, N., and Saxton, J. (1987). *Teaching Drama: A Mind of Many Wonders*, Hutchinson Education

Ogilvie, K. (1993). *Leading and Managing Groups in the Outdoors*, NAOE Publications

Ornstein, R. (1977). *The Psychology of Consciousness*, Penguin

Orr, D. (1994). *Earth in Mind: On Education, Environment and the Human Prospect*, Island Press

O'Toole, J. (1992). *Process of Drama. Negotiating Art and Meaning*, Routledge

Pike, G., and Selby, D. (1989). *Global Teacher, Global Learner*, Hodder and Stoughton

Purves, L. (1996). Afraid of Adventure, *The Times*, 21.5.96

Randle, D. (1989). *Teaching Green*, Green Print

Repp, G. (1996). Outdoor adventure education and Friluftsliv seen from a sociology of knowledge perspective, *Journal of Adventure Education and Outdoor Leadership*, 13 (2)

Rogers, A. (Ed.) (1990). *EARTHworks: The Action Pack*, Council for Environmental Education

Sax, J. (1980). *Mountains without Handrails*, University of Michigan

Sidaway, R. (1988). *Sport, Recreation and Nature Conservation*, The Sports Council and Countryside Commission

Sterling, S. and Cooper, G. (1992). *In Touch—Environmental Education for Europe*, WWF (UK)

Tellnes, A. (1993). Friluftsliv—Outdoor nature life as a method to change attitudes, *Journal of Adventure Education and Outdoor Leadership*, 10 (3)

Van Matre, S. (1972). *Acclimatization*, American Camping Association

Van Matre, S. (1974). *Acclimatizing*, American Camping Association

Van Matre, S. (1990). *Earth Education: A New Beginning*, Institute for Earth Education

Van Matre, S., and Johnson, B. (1997). *Sunship III—Perception and Choice for the Journey Ahead*, Institute for Earth Education

Wagner B. J. (1979). *Dorothy Heathcote, Drama as a Learning Medium*, Hutchinson Education

Woods, P. (1993). *Critical Events in Teaching and Learning*, The Falmer Press

Useful addresses

Adventure and Environmental Awareness Group
Low Bank Ground, Coniston, Cumbria, LA21 8AA
Tel: 015394 41314
This is a forum for those interested in the links between outdoor recreation, education and conservation. It runs occasional conferences and training workshops on current issues.

Adventure Education
12 St. Andrew's Churchyard, Penrith, Cumbria, CA11 7YE
Tel: 01768 891065
A not-for-profit organisation providing professional services to the outdoor education field in the UK. Publishes the *Journal of Adventure Education and Outdoor Leadership* and also the *Outdoor Source Book*.

British Trust for Conservation Volunteers (BTCV)
36 St. Mary's Street, Wallingford, Oxon OX10 0EU
Tel: 01491 839766
Introduces people of all ages to practical conservation projects. Offers cheap working holidays and local one day projects for people aged 16+. Also provides publications and training for leaders.

Common Ground
Seven Dials Warehouse, 44 Earlham Street, London WC2H 9LA
Tel: 0171 3793109
The organisation has for many years inspired community, environment and arts projects including tree dressing and creating parish maps.

Council for Environmental Education (CEE)
University of Reading, London Road, Reading, RG1 5AQ
Tel: 0138 9756061
The national co-ordinating body in England and Wales for environmental education. Its Youth Unit produces resources and a regular newsletter, *EARTHlines*, as well as running its own environmental youth work programme.

Duke of Edinburgh's Award
Gulliver House, Madeira Walk, Windsor, Berks SL4 1EU
Tel: 01753 810753
There are opportunities for young people aged 14–25 years to explore the environment and take part in conservation projects as part of the Award scheme.

Field Studies Council
Preston Montford, Montford Bridge, Shrewsbury, SY4 1DX
Tel: 01743 850674
Has 13 centres offering courses in fieldwork and environmental education and a range of scientific publications.

Foundation for Outdoor Adventure
St. Michael's Nook, Muncaster, Ravenglass, Cumbria, CA18 1RD
Tel: 01229 717170
An educational charity set up to promote opportunities for outdoor adventure for young people.

Friends of the Earth
26–28 Underwood Street, London, N1 7TQ
Tel: 0171 4901555
Campaigning organisation to promote more sustainable lifestyles. It produces information on environmental issues and has many local branches.

Groundwork Foundation
85–87 Cornwall Street, Birmingham, B3 3BY
Tel: 0121 236 8565
Can give information on local Groundwork Trusts which work in partnerships to improve environments. Some Trusts are involved in projects with young people.

John Muir Trust
12 Wellington Place, Leith, Scotland, EH6 7EQ
Tel: 0131 5540114
The Trust manages several extensive wild areas in Scotland and also runs an environmental award scheme for young people.

Learning through Landscapes
Southside Offices, The Law Courts, Winchester, SO23 9DL
Tel: 01962 846258
Its main aim is to help teachers with ideas for improving school grounds but it produces a good range of environmental resources.

National Association for Environmental Education
University of Wolverhampton, Gorway, Walsall, WS1 3BD
Tel: 01922 31200
The main professional organisation for environmental education. It produces a regular magazine, *Environmental Education*, holds conferences and publishes occasional papers.

National Association for Outdoor Education
12 St. Andrew's Churchyard, Penrith, Cumbria, CA11 7YE
Tel: 01768 865113
The main professional organisation for outdoor education. Produces the *Journal of Aventure Education and Outdoor Leadership*, in conjunction with Adventure Education and the Association of Heads of Outdoor Education Centres.

National Association of Field Studies Officers
Stibbington Centre for Environmental Education, Great North Road, Stibbington, Peterborough PE8 6LP
Tel: 01780 782386
The professional organisation for field studies. It produces a directory of field studies and environmental education centres.

Rescue Mission UK
White House, Buntingford, Herts., SG9 9AH
Tel: 01763 274459
UK based international organisation encouraging young people to participate in Agenda 21.

Royal Society for the Protection of Birds
The Lodge, Sandy, Beds., SG19 2DL
Tel: 01767 680551
Manages a variety of bird reserves and produces outdoor teaching materials and a regular magazine for members. RSPB Phoenix is the environmental club for 13–19 year olds. The organisation has become involved in wider aspects of environmental education.

Scottish Environmental Education Council (SEEC)
University of Stirling, Stirling, FK9 4LA
Tel: 01786 467867
The co-ordinating body for environmental education in Scotland.

Scottish Natural Heritage
Battleby, Redgorton, Perth, PH1 3EW
Tel: 01738 627921
This is the government body responsible for the conservation of Scotland's natural heritage. It has an active education branch which produces resources and supports environmental education initiatives. It recognises the important link between outdoor and environmental education.

Tidy Britain Group
The Pier, Wigan, WN3 4EX
Tel: 01942 824620
This national organisation produces environmental resources mainly for schools. Eco-Schools project has useful ideas for environmental audits.

Wildlife Trusts
The Green, Witham Park, Waterside South, Lincoln LN5 2JR
Tel: 01522 544400
The national organisation for local wildlife trusts. The junior wing, WATCH, organises many national environmental projects undertaken by young people.

WWF
Panda House, Weyside Park, Godalming, Surrey, GU71XR
Tel: 01483 426444
This is the largest nature conservation organisation active around the world. WWF (UK) has an excellent reputation for its educational work and publications for teachers, leaders and young people. It has initiated projects to encourage young people to become involved in Local Agenda 21 issues.